EXPLORE THE BIBLE
BOOK BY BOOK

PETER MARTIN

LION

CONTENTS

INTRODUCTION — 4

THE OLD TESTAMENT — 6

GENESIS (1–11) — 8

GENESIS (12–50) — 10

EXODUS (1–15) — 12

EXODUS (16–24) — 14

EXODUS (25–40) — 16

LEVITICUS & NUMBERS — 18

DEUTERONOMY — 20

JOSHUA — 22

JUDGES — 24

RUTH — 26

1 SAMUEL — 28

2 SAMUEL — 30

1 KINGS (1–11) — 32

1 KINGS (12–22) — 34

2 KINGS — 36

KINGS & PROPHETS OF THE OLD TESTAMENT — 38

2 KINGS (1–20) — 40

2 KINGS (21–25) — 42

1 & 2 CHRONICLES — 44

EZRA — 46

NEHEMIAH — 47

ESTHER — 48

JOB — 50

PSALMS (1–106) — 52

PSALMS (107–150) — 54

PROVERBS — 56

ECCLESIASTES — 58

SONG OF SONGS — 59

ISAIAH (1–39) — 60

ISAIAH (40–55) — 62

ISAIAH (56–65) — 64

JEREMIAH 1 — 66

JEREMIAH 2 — 68

LAMENTATIONS — 69

EZEKIEL — 70

DANIEL — 72

HOSEA — 74

JOEL — 75

AMOS — 76

OBADIAH — 77

JONAH (1–2) — 78

JONAH (3–4) — 80

MICAH — 81

NAHUM — 82

HABAKKUK — 83

ZEPHANIAH — 84

HAGGAI — 85

ZECHARIAH — 86

MALACHI — 87

THE SCRIPTURES COME INTO BEING — 88

THE SCRIPTURES IN GREEK — 90

THE DEUTEROCANON — 92

1 & 2 MACCABEES — 94

THE NEW TESTAMENT — 96

MATTHEW 1 — 98

MATTHEW 2 — 100

MARK — 102

LUKE 1 — 104

LUKE 2 — 106

PARABLES — 107

JOHN 1 — 108

JOHN 2 — 110

ACTS — 112

PAUL'S TRAVELS — 114

LETTERS FROM CHRISTIANS — 116

ROMANS — 118

1 CORINTHIANS — 120

2 CORINTHIANS — 121

GALATIANS — 122

EPHESIANS — 124

PHILIPPIANS — 126

COLOSSIANS — 128

PHILEMON — 129

1 & 2 THESSALONIANS — 130

1 TIMOTHY — 132

2 TIMOTHY — 133

TITUS — 134

PHILEMON — 135

LETTER TO THE HEBREWS — 136

JAMES — 138

1 PETER — 140

2 PETER — 141

1, 2, & 3 JOHN — 142

JUDE — 143

REVELATION — 144

THE CHRISTIAN BIBLE — 146

TRANSLATING THE BIBLE — 148

TELLING THE BIBLE — 150

ALL OVER THE WORLD — 152

READING THE BIBLE — 154

INDEX — 156

THE BOOKS OF THE BIBLE: QUICK FINDER — 158

ACKNOWLEDGMENTS — 160

INTRODUCTION

What is the Bible?

The Bible is the book at the heart of the Christian faith: the Scriptures.

All over the world, Christians are eager to explore what the Bible says. They would agree with the following words, which were written by one of the very first Christians. He, Paul, wrote them in a letter to a newer Christian named Timothy to encourage him to study the Scriptures. As the Good News Bible states:

All Scripture is inspired by God and is useful for teaching the truth, rebuking error, correcting faults, and giving instruction for right living, so that the person who serves God may be fully qualified and equipped to do every kind of good deed.

2 Timothy 3:16–17

Where does the Bible come from?

The Christian Bible is not a single book: it contains two very different collections of writings. Christians refer to them as the Old Testament and the New Testament. The word "testament" means "covenant". It refers to the promise God makes to people that is at the heart of the faith.

Each collection has many books within it. The word "Bible" comes from the Greek word *biblia* and simply means "the books". All the books that Christians have come to regard as helpful to their faith are bound together as this single volume.

BCE and CE

"BCE" (Before the Christian Era) covers all the time before the year 1, and is equivalent to BC (Before Christ).

"CE" (Christian Era) indicates the period after the year 1, and is equivalent to AD (Anno Domini, the Latin for "in the year of the Lord").

The Old Testament

The books that Christians have gathered to make the Old Testament are the Scriptures of the Jewish faith. They are sometimes called the Hebrew Bible, as they were for the most part written in Hebrew, which from ancient times, was the language of the Jewish people. The collection of writings from which the Old Testament was selected was put together around 2,300 years ago (see pages 90–91 on Greek translation/the Septuagint).

The books are all very different. For example, there are books of laws, books of history, stories, poems, proverbs, and the sayings of holy men known as prophets.

The New Testament

The New Testament contains writings from the early days of the Christian faith. The most revered are the four accounts of the life of Jesus – the one whom Christians follow. These accounts are known as the Gospels. There is also an account of how Jesus' followers spread their new faith (Acts of the Apostles) as well as letters from Christians written to help new believers.

These books were written in Greek, in the fifty years or so following the life of Jesus. That means the books are nearly 2,000 years old.

Above, right: An example of a parchment scroll. This is one of many scrolls that were discovered in caves at Qumran near the Dead Sea in 1947 (see page 89). The Isaiah Scroll dates from 100 BCE and is the oldest complete copy of the book of Isaiah.

Original manuscript

The Bible has been put together from writings that are very old indeed. However, even the very oldest versions that people can see today are copies. Both Jews and Christians treasured their Scriptures and copied them out by hand – on parchment scrolls and sheets of papyrus – so that the words would not be lost.

The ancient scrolls discovered at Qumran would have been placed in tall clay jars like this one to protect the text and to preserve them. Also shown here is a fragment of a scroll that was discovered there.

Chapter and verse

If you look at a modern Bible it will be quite different from the oldest manuscripts. For one thing, you are likely to see a Bible that has been translated into your language (the Bible has now been translated into almost every language in the world). For another, each of the books has been divided into "chapters" and "verses" so that readers can follow their way round the text more easily. The chapter divisions were added long after Bible times. You can read about the early translations on pages 148–49 under Translating the Bible.

Book	Chapter	Verse
John	**3**	**16**

A scene showing the first-century CE Jewish religious community at Qumran hiding the scrolls of Scripture in clay jars before placing them in the caves by the Dead Sea so as to protect them from the advancing Romans.

THE OLD TESTAMENT

The books of the Old Testament are categorized into five sections.

GENESIS EXODUS LEVITICUS NUMBERS DEUTERONOMY

Pentateuch

JOSHUA JUDGES RUTH 1 SAMUEL 2 SAMUEL 1 KINGS 2 KINGS 1 CHRONICLES 2 CHRONICLES EZRA NEHEMIAH ESTHER

History books

Pentateuch

This is the name given to the first five books of the Bible. Jews refer to them as "the Book of the Law" or the "Torah".

There is an ancient tradition that Moses was the author of these books. Some experts question this: they argue that scholars in later times looked back at the old stories of their people and mixed them with their own retellings and interpretations. Either way, Moses remains the key prophet of the people of Israel and the laws at the heart of their covenant with God.

The books are not just lists of laws, however. They contain ancient stories that show the relationship between God and the world, and between God and the very beginnings of the people of Israel, who were later to be known as the Jews.

History books

These books give an account of the unfolding drama of the people of Israel. Some of the books are about the people as they attempt to make their home in the land of Canaan and to establish themselves as a nation. After hundreds of years of struggle they are spectacularly defeated and many are forced to live in exile.

In ancient times, the Scriptures would have been read aloud to gatherings such as this one. People were keen to learn more about God and to understand the laws that had been set out for them.

JOB	PSALMS	PROVERBS	ECCLESIASTES	SONG OF SONGS	ISAIAH	JEREMIAH	LAMENTATIONS	EZEKIEL	DANIEL	HOSEA	JOEL	AMOS	OBADIAH	JONAH	MICAH	NAHUM	HABAKKUK	ZEPHANIAH	HAGGAI	ZECHARIAH	MALACHI

Poetry and wisdom   **Major prophets**   **Minor prophets**

The later history books deal with events as the people return to their land after the exile. The books known as 1 and 2 Chronicles were written in this later period to give a fresh interpretation of the older events.

Poetry and wisdom

Psalms is a book of Hebrew verse that contains prayers and hymns, while the Song of Songs (also known as the Song of Solomon) is a love poem.

In different ways the wisdom books try to answer the difficult questions of life: why are things the way they are and what is the best way to live to deal with life's problems?

Prophets

The prophets of Old Testament times were people who were credited with having a special relationship with God that enabled them to speak God's truth to the people. The books include words of warning for wrongdoing and exhortation to righteousness.

Time and again the people failed to live by God's standards, the prophets warned. Would they ever be able to live as God's people should? As the disappointments grew, the prophets brought hope: that one day God would send a rescuer – a chosen king, a messiah.

The books of Isaiah, Jeremiah (said to be the author of Lamentations), Ezekiel, and Daniel are classed as having been written by "major prophets". Their portraits, shown left, are found in a twelfth-century monastery in Cyprus.

These books are usually split into two and are labelled "major prophets" and "minor prophets" – not because the major prophets are necessarily more important, but rather due to their longer length.

GENESIS (1–11)

Genesis is the first book in the Bible. The word itself means "origin", and Genesis is about the very beginnings of everything.

Chapters 1–11 contain ancient stories that explain why the world is the way it is.

The creation

It begins with an account of God calling the world into being from out of a dark, chaotic nothingness. At the end of creation God considers the result:

God looked at everything he had made, and he was very pleased.

Genesis 1:31

GENESIS

EXODUS

LEVITICUS

NUMBERS

DEUTERONOMY

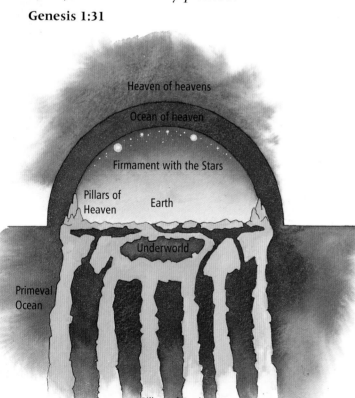

Heaven of heavens

Ocean of heaven

Firmament with the Stars

Pillars of Heaven

Earth

Underworld

Primeval Ocean

Pillars of Earth

The account of creation in Genesis says that in the beginning there was chaos, which is likened to a primeval ocean. It is from this chaos that God creates the world: light, sea, and sky (Genesis 1:1–10). This diagram shows how this division may have been viewed.

Adam and Eve

Human beings are the pinnacle of all that God has made. In the story of the first people – Adam and Eve – the world is a paradise garden that provides them with all they need. They simply gather their food from what grows around them. God tells them that they should live this innocent life and enjoy their maker's friendship. However, they choose to know about bad things as well as good things. Because of that choice, they have to say goodbye to their simple lives as gatherers. Instead, they have to work the land themselves to have enough to survive on.

Cain and Abel

The firstborn sons of Adam and Eve – Cain and Abel – also make a living from the land. Cain is a farmer who grows crops. Abel is a shepherd. Cain allows himself to become jealous of his younger brother and murders him (see picture below). This is just one example of the anger and violence that takes root in humankind.

Noah

The world becomes so wicked that God decides to make a fresh start. He chooses Noah to build an ark. That way he can protect his family and a breeding pair of every kind of animal from a worldwide flood.

When the waters go down, God makes a promise, or a "covenant":

Never again will I put the earth under a curse because of what people do; I know that from the time they are young their thoughts are evil. Never again will I destroy all living beings, as I have done this time. As long as the world exists, there will be a time for planting and a time for harvest. There will always be cold and heat, summer and winter, day and night.

Genesis 8:21–22

God's promise

The sign of God's promise to Noah and his family was the rainbow.

The Tower of Babylon

This story tells of a time when people all spoke the same language. They worked together to build a city with a great tower that would reach to heaven. God was displeased at their arrogance. He mixed up their languages so they could not work together. The building was abandoned and the people went their separate ways. That was the beginning of the many language groups all over the world.

The story of the Tower of Babylon is linked to the ruins of a temple tower in the ancient city of Babylon. Although the story is set in very ancient times, it would have had special meaning for the people of Israel when they lived in exile. Read about this on page 45.

GENESIS (12–50)

The second part of Genesis is about the family that became the people of Israel.

Abraham, Isaac, and Jacob

The father of them all is a man named Abram, whom God later renames Abraham.

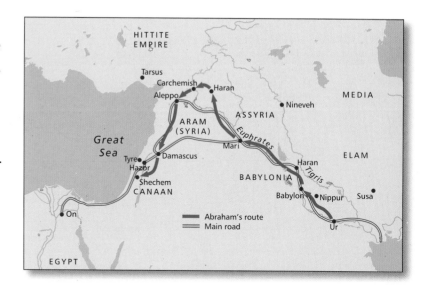

The Lord said to Abram, "Leave your country, your relatives, and your father's home, and go to a land that I am going to show you. I will give you many descendants, and they will become a great nation. I will bless you and make your name famous, so that you will be a blessing."

Genesis 12:1–2

So it is that Abraham settles in the land of Canaan. He and his wife Sarah have a son: Isaac. Isaac and his wife Rebekah have twin sons, Jacob and Esau. It is the younger, Jacob, who claims the rights of the firstborn and whose descendants will be the nation God will bless.

On God's command, Abraham and Sarah, together with Abraham's nephew, Lot, their servants, flocks, and herds, left Ur in the east and travelled hundreds of miles to Canaan in the west. The map above shows their journey.

The covenant with Abraham

God's promise to (or "covenant" with) Abraham is part of a plan: to rebuild the relationship between God and his people that was broken when humankind chose wickedness.

Joseph and his brothers

Jacob – later named Israel – has twelve sons. He chooses Joseph, the youngest but the firstborn of his favourite wife Rachel, to have the rights of the firstborn. This makes the older brothers angry. In a sudden burst of rage they sell Joseph to be a slave in Egypt.

God continues to take care of Joseph when he is in Egypt. God enables him to explain dreams, and Joseph predicts a famine. The king of Egypt, the pharaoh, puts him in charge of storing grain to last through the lean years. Eventually, Joseph's brothers come pleading to buy food.

Joseph comes to understand that everything that happened is part of God's plan. He invites his family to leave Canaan and come to Egypt, where they can live in safety.

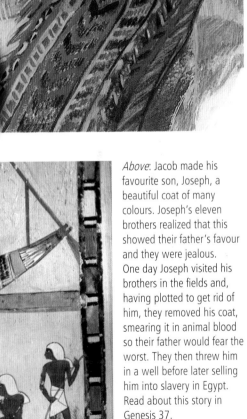

Rights of the firstborn

The firstborn son was the one who normally received a double inheritance, and who would inherit his father's role as head of the family.

Above: Jacob made his favourite son, Joseph, a beautiful coat of many colours. Joseph's eleven brothers realized that this showed their father's favour and they were jealous. One day Joseph visited his brothers in the fields and, having plotted to get rid of him, they removed his coat, smearing it in animal blood so their father would fear the worst. They then threw him in a well before later selling him into slavery in Egypt. Read about this story in Genesis 37.

Left: This ancient Egyptian wall painting shows the collection and storing of grain as it might have happened in Joseph's day.

EXODUS (1–15)

The book of Exodus is the second book of the Bible.

It continues the story of the descendants of Abraham, Isaac, and Jacob begun in Genesis.

The people have prospered in Egypt. Children and grandchildren have been born, generation after generation. Now they are so many they are a nation. They are sometimes called the Hebrews and sometimes the people of Israel.

Slaves in Egypt

A new king of Egypt, the pharaoh, comes to power. He knows nothing of Joseph. The pharaoh is afraid the Israelites will cause trouble in his land. He makes them his slaves and orders his soldiers to seek out all newborn baby boys and throw them in the River Nile.

A mother hides her baby in a floating cradle by the water's edge. A royal princess finds him and adopts him. She names him "Moses".

Moses

Moses grows up in safety, but he knows he is really one of the slave people. As a young man he challenges one of the Egyptian slave masters, gets into a fight, and kills him. In fear for his life, he escapes to the wild country and begins a new life as a shepherd. He is helped by a man named Jethro, whose daughter he marries.

Years later, on a mountain known as Sinai, he sees a bush on fire but not burning. There, in the presence of this miracle, God speaks to him and tells him to lead his people to freedom. This means leading them from Egypt to the land of Canaan, the land God had shown Abraham.

Moses is given permission to ask his brother to help him go and face the pharaoh and ask for the people of Israel's release. The king clearly does not care anything about the God of his slaves and says no.

Plagues

The disasters that God sent to Egypt as a punishment are also known as "plagues" and included everything from hordes of frogs to boils that affected the people and their animals.

Exodus 7:14 – 12:36

Passover

Moses predicted that God would send one disaster after another. The final disaster God sent to Egypt was the death of their firstborn. Moses told the people to prepare a last meal in Egypt: bread without yeast and a roast lamb. They were to mark their doors with the blood of the lamb. The angel of death would see the mark and "pass over" their homes. This event was to be remembered in the festival of Passover for ever, and it centred (and continues to centre) on a shared meal.

The fleeing Israelites would have been fearful of the powerful Egyptian army that would have been chasing them in speeding chariots like this example.

After that the king let Moses' people go. Then he changed his mind and sent an army after them to get them back.

In a miracle, that the people remembered for ever as a symbol of God's power and protection, God makes a way through the sea for his people so they can walk to safety. The Egyptian army is drowned as the sea returns.

> I will sing to the Lord, because he has won a
>   glorious victory;
> he has thrown the horses and their riders into
>   the sea.
> The Lord is my strong defender;
>   he is the one who has saved me.
> He is my God, and I will praise him,
>   my father's God, and I will sing about his
>   greatness.
>
> Faithful to your promise, you led the people you
>   had rescued;
> by your strength you guided them to your sacred
>   land.

Exodus 15:1–2, 13

Moses leads the Israelites out of slavery in Egypt toward Canaan. Their great escape is known as the exodus.

EXODUS (16–24)

Moses leads his people out of slavery and toward a land they can make their home. There is a brief moment of celebration.

In the wilderness

The region between Egypt and Canaan is wild country: dry, rocky, barren. Almost at once, the people begin to complain. They remember the good things they had in Egypt, such as their productive vegetable plots, and are angry to find themselves in a harsh and barren wilderness.

God provides for them. Drinkable water appears in unlikely places; quail simply drop out of the air and can be caught for food. A flaky white substance appears each morning on the ground: this they call manna, and it is good to eat.

Manna

At first, the Israelites weren't sure what the food was that God had provided, so they named it "manna", meaning "What is it?"

Even so, Moses is kept very busy dealing with all the arguments in the camp. His father-in-law, Jethro, advises him to appoint judges to do this work.

Moses and God's commandments

The people come to Mount Sinai. There, Moses tells them, God will make himself known.

Even as the mountain is hidden in cloud, as the thunder roars and lightning flashes, Moses climbs alone to the summit.

When he returns, he brings a set of commandments: God's laws for God's people. They are written on stone.

Lightning strikes over Mount Sinai.

The traditional site of Mount Sinai, also called Mount Horeb in the Bible, is thought to be that of modern-day Jebel Musa.

Law and covenant

There were many other laws besides the great ten. They spoke in detail about how to show respect for God and how to show respect for other people. They were at the heart of a promise – a covenant. If the people would obey God's laws, then God would bless them. They would be able to settle in the land of Canaan and live there in peace and prosperity.

The stone tablets on which the great laws were written were to be kept safe, in a box covered with gold. This was the ark of the covenant. It was fitted with poles so that it could be carried in procession without anyone touching it.

God spoke, and these were his words:

"I am the Lord your God who brought you out of Egypt, where you were slaves.
Worship no god but me.
Do not make for yourselves images of anything in heaven or on earth or in the water under the earth. Do not bow down to any idol or worship it…
Do not use my name for evil purposes…
Observe the Sabbath and keep it holy. … In six days I, the Lord, made the earth, the sky, the seas, and everything in them, but on the seventh day I rested. That is why I, the Lord, blessed the Sabbath and made it holy.
Respect your father and your mother, so that you may live a long time in the land that I am giving you.
Do not commit murder.
Do not commit adultery.
Do not steal.
Do not accuse anyone falsely.
Do not desire another man's house; do not desire his wife, his slaves, his cattle, his donkeys, or anything else that he owns."

Exodus 20:1–17 (see also Deuteronomy 5:1–21)

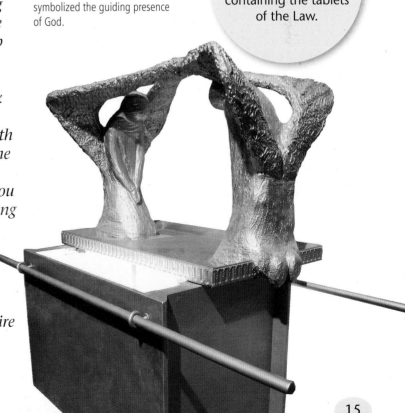

A model of the ark of the covenant. Over the top was the "mercy seat", which had two gold cherubim with wings. They symbolized the guiding presence of God.

Ark of the covenant

A wooden chest containing the tablets of the Law.

EXODUS (25–40)

The final chapters of Exodus deal with instructions for worship. Once again, Moses acts as God's messenger. The instructions are designed for a people who are living as nomads.

The tabernacle

The place of worship is to be a tent, just as the people's homes are tents. However, it will be a special tent crafted skilfully from fine materials. It is called the tabernacle.

It will have an inner room and an outer room.

The inner room, the Holy of Holies, is where the Law at the heart of the covenant is to be treasured, in a golden box: the ark of the covenant (see also pages 14–15, Exodus 16–24).

In the outer room is an altar on which incense is to be burned, and a lampstand for seven lamps that are to be kept burning.

Wherever the tabernacle is set up, it must be screened within a courtyard. In the courtyard there is to be a huge basin of water so the priests can "purify" themselves by washing, and an altar where offerings to God can be burned.

Altar
A structure used in worship on which a gift or sacrifice was offered to God.

Below is a modern reconstruction of the tabernacle, which was a portable tent or "dwelling" in which God was worshipped during the forty years that the Israelites were wandering in the wilderness (see Exodus 25:8).

The bronze **altar** was used to offer sacrifices to God.

The **outer court.**

The bronze **laver** (basin) was used by priests for washing before they offered sacrifices to God.

The **Holy of Holies**, an inner room at the back of the tabernacle, containing the ark of the covenant. Only the high priest could enter here once a year on the Day of Atonement (Yom Kippur) to sacrifice for his and the nation's sins.

Exodus 25:8 and 29:45–46

The golden calf

The account of the building of the tabernacle is interrupted with a dreadful set back: while Moses is on Mount Sinai, the people feel abandoned. They ask Aaron to make them a golden bull calf that they can worship as a god. When it is produced, the celebrations are wild and wicked.

Moses returns to the frenzy. In a fury he breaks the stone tablets on which the laws are written and punishes the wrongdoers. Even so, God is willing to forgive the people. A second set of tablets are cut and the covenant is renewed (Exodus 33, 34).

An artist's impression of Moses destroying the golden calf.

Only the high priest (left) was allowed to enter the Holy of Holies. Over his blue robe he wore a breastplate containing twelve precious stones, each one engraved with the name of the twelve tribes of Israel (see Exodus 28). The ordinary priest would wear the much more simple white linen robe.

LEVITICUS & NUMBERS

Leviticus is the third book of the Bible, and of the so-called Pentateuch.

It is sometimes called "the book of the priests", and it contains instructions, rules, and regulations. Some of these are about the right way to worship God. Others are about how people should treat one another.

One of the central themes that is repeated throughout the book is the holiness of God and the expectation that the people of God will also be holy; Leviticus 19:2 says, "Be holy, because I… am holy."

The book of Numbers is also part of the Pentateuch. Its name comes from the fact that it tells of two occasions when Moses conducts a census of the people – literally counting them.

The best-known verse from Leviticus is 19:18:

"love your neighbours as you love yourself."

This is one of the two great laws that Jesus himself said was at the heart of right living.

Matthew 22:39; Mark 12:31

Forty years in the wilderness

The main story is about the majority of the forty years the nation spent in the wilderness between Egypt and Canaan. It tells of how they reached the border of Canaan quite quickly after their escape from Egypt. Moses sent twelve brave young warriors as spies to find out more about what the land was like, but their report was mixed.

On the good side, it was very fertile. As proof the spies cut a bunch of grapes so big that the only way to carry it was slung from a pole carried between two people.

On the discouraging side, the spies reported that its people lived in well-defended walled cities that would be hard to attack. Other war-like tribes also lived in Canaan, and their warriors were giants compared with the people of Israel.

Two of the spies – Joshua and Caleb – were eager to go and claim Canaan.

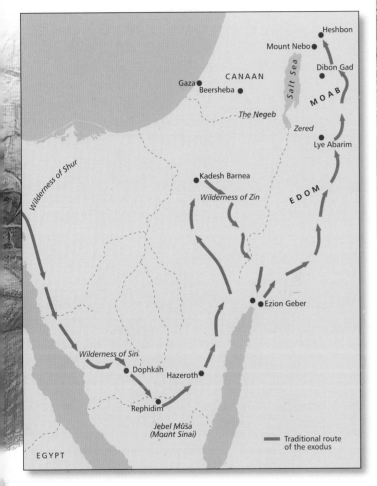

From Mount Nebo, which overlooked the Dead Sea and Jordan Valley, Moses was able to view the land of Canaan.

Their confidence was not enough to convince the people. They spent many more years as nomads in the wilderness, often harassed by other tribes, before they dared make a second attempt.

In the closing chapters of Numbers, God tells Moses to appoint Joshua, who will be the next leader of the nation. God also gives more rules and regulations to the people as they wait on the plains of Moab, on the eastern side of the Jordan, for the right moment to enter Canaan.

The land we explored is an excellent land. If the Lord is pleased with us, he will take us there and give us that rich and fertile land.

Numbers 14:7–8

Map: The long journey the Israelites undertook to reach Canaan. From Egypt they journeyed south to Mount Sinai before heading north toward Mount Nebo, from which Canaan could be seen.
Left: The spies discovered that the Canaanite people were defended by strong fortresses with high walls.

DEUTERONOMY

This is the fifth and final book in the Pentateuch. The name comes from a Greek word meaning "second law". The first Law was the one given to Moses at Mount Sinai (Exodus 19:16 – 20:21). Since then, the people have glimpsed the land of Canaan but dared not claim it, choosing instead to live as nomads in the wilderness. Now they are camped on the plains of Moab, getting ready to enter Canaan.

The first and greatest commandment

Moses tells them the Law for a second time. Among his sermons are the words that Jesus declared to be the first and greatest commandment:

> *Israel, remember this! The Lord – and the Lord alone – is our God. Love the Lord your God with all your heart, with all your soul, and with all your strength.*
> **Deuteronomy 6:4–5 (see also Matthew 22:36–38)**

God's laws

The people are instructed to remember God's laws, to obey them, and to teach their children to do the same. If they do, then God will bless them. They will be successful in making their claim for the land of Canaan and will live there in peace and prosperity for always.

> *Remember these commands and cherish them. Tie them on your arms and wear them on your foreheads as a reminder. Teach them to your children. Talk about them when you are at home and when you are away, when you are resting and when you are working. Write them on the doorposts of your houses and on your gates. Then you and your children will live a long time in the land that the Lord your God promised to give your ancestors.*
> **Deuteronomy 11:18–21**

Modern Jews today continue to wear "phylacteries" on their foreheads – small black boxes containing parchments including the words from Deuteronomy 6:4–9 on them (above).

Festivals

The Pentateuch is full of instructions for how to celebrate the great religious festivals. Deuteronomy names three in particular:

Passover

The festival to remember the escape from Egypt (Exodus 12). On this occasion, the people are to make bread without yeast (see page 12).

Harvest

The harvest festival was to be held seven weeks after the start of the harvest and was a time to bring offerings to God. By the time of Jesus this festival was known as Pentecost.

Shelters

The festival of shelters (or of tabernacles; see Leviticus 23:33–44) was to be held after the grapes had been pressed for wine. It was to be a celebration for the nation and for everyone in the community, including any foreigners. It came to be a time when families went out into the forest to gather branches with which to build simple shelters – a reminder of their time as nomads in the wilderness. At the same time, they enjoyed a feast that reminded them of the blessing of being settlers in the land of Canaan (Nehemiah 9:24).

Death of Moses

The final chapter, 34, tells of the death of Moses. He goes to the top of Mount Nebo (see page 19) and from that point God shows far more than the eye can see – the whole of the land of Canaan that God has promised the people of Abraham, Isaac, and Jacob: the people of Israel. There he dies. His body is collected and buried with great honour.

There has never been a prophet in Israel like Moses; the Lord spoke with him face-to-face.

Deuteronomy 34:10

Ever since that first Passover, Jewish families have gathered together to celebrate their being saved from the plague of the death of the firstborn. During a family meal, the story of the Israelites' escape from Egypt is retold.

JOSHUA

The book of Joshua continues the story of the people of Israel after the death of Moses. Under his leadership they prepare to enter Canaan and then make it their home.

History books

- JOSHUA
- JUDGES
- RUTH
- 1 SAMUEL
- 2 SAMUEL
- 1 KINGS
- 2 KINGS
- 1 CHRONICLES
- 2 CHRONICLES
- EZRA
- NEHEMIAH
- ESTHER

Obeying the Law

God makes this promise to Joshua:

Just be determined, be confident; and make sure that you obey the whole Law that my servant Moses gave you. Do not neglect any part of it and you will succeed wherever you go.

Joshua 1:7

Jericho and the conquest

Joshua makes plans for the invasion of Canaan. The first city they reach is Jericho (Joshua 5:13 – 6:27). The people see that it is strongly defended and they lose heart. God tells Joshua to march in procession round the city for six days. Part of the procession is the ark of the covenant, carried by priests. It is a sign that God's laws are central to the Israelite campaign.

The seventh day of marching is the final one. With trumpets sounding, and on a sign from Joshua, the people give a great shout. The city walls fall down. It is the first of many miracles that enable Joshua to lead the people to victory.

Land to live on

When they finally capture the land Joshua decides how it is to be divided up among the great families – the tribes of Israel. They no longer need to live as nomads. They can farm the land.

A reminder of the covenant

The years go by. When Joshua is very old he calls the people together to remind them of the terms of the covenant: God's promise to give them the land of Canaan and the promise they made to obey the Law. Joshua said:

Now then… honour the Lord and serve him sincerely and faithfully. Get rid of the gods which your ancestors used to worship in Mesopotamia and in Egypt, and serve only the Lord. If you are not willing to serve him, decide today whom you will serve, the gods your ancestors worshipped in Mesopotamia or the gods of the Amorites, in whose land you are now living. As for my family and me, we will serve the Lord.

Joshua 24:14–15

Map shows the land as it was divided among the twelve tribes of Israel (shown in upper case).

Left: Families ploughing the land on which they have settled, making it their own.

Far left: Priests and warriors outside the walls of Jericho.

JUDGES

The book of Judges describes the period in the history of Israel from the settlement of the land under Joshua to just before the time of the last judge, Samuel.

Enemies all around

The book describes the difficulties facing the nation. The Israelites have claimed the land but they haven't driven out the Canaanites, and the relationship between the two nations is uneasy.

Also, there are other nations living on the edge of the land who are always eager to come plundering whenever they see a chance.

When Joshua dies, the Israelites are tempted to worship the gods of other nations. This, Judges says, is the root of every disaster.

They stopped worshipping the Lord and served the Baals and the Astartes. And so the Lord became furious with Israel and let raiders attack and rob them.

Judges 2:13–14

Judges

From time to time God would give the people a leader who would drive out their enemies and insist that they worship God. These twelve leaders are the "judges" of the book's title. As soon as each leader died, however, the people would go back to their bad old ways.

Judges
Othniel, Ehud, Shamgar – chapter 3
Deborah/Barak – chapters 4–5
Gideon – chapters 6–8
Tola, Jair – chapter 10
Jephthah – chapters 10–12
Ibzan, Elon, and Abdon – chapter 12
Samson – chapters 13–16

The Israelites, led by judges Deborah and Barak, overcame Canaanite king Jabin's powerful army led by Sisera. Fighting with only swords and spears, God was with the Israelites and they won the battle when the River Kishon overflowed, sinking Sisera's 900 mighty iron chariots.

God's gift to Samson was his powerful strength – symbolized in his long hair. When his hair is cut off, he loses his strength. Having spent time in prison, his hair, along with his strength, begins to grow again, and with God's help, he is able to push aside the pillars of the Temple, thus destroying the Philistine enemy (Judges 16).

There are other judges whose stories are told in 1 Samuel. There is Eli, whose sons are not worthy of the role. Instead God chooses Samuel to be the leader of Israel. Samuel's sons Joel and Abijah command so little respect the people ask for a king to rule them (1 Samuel 4, 7, 8).

Dramatic stories

The stories of the great leaders in the book of Judges are some of the most dramatic in the Bible. Among them are Deborah, who leads the people to victory against the Canaanite king Jabin; Gideon, who defeats the raiding Midianites; and Samson, who wages a one-man war against the Philistines.

The time of the judges is one of almost unending warring and violence. The people of Israel are far from living as God's laws require.

Baal and Astarte

Baal was the name of the Canaanite god. His followers believed he controlled the weather and the fertility of the land. The Israelites relied on good harvests, and they must have been tempted to copy the Canaanites and so keep the local god on their side. Astarte (or Asherah) was Baal's goddess partner.

Bronze figurines of the Canaanite goddess Astarte (left) and god Baal (right).

RUTH

The story of Ruth is set in the time of the judges, and shows a much more appealing and peaceable side of the times.

A foreigner

Ruth is a foreigner – a Moabite. She comes to the land of Israel out of loyalty to her mother-in-law Naomi, who has no other family after her husband and two grown-up sons die. Ruth tells Naomi:

Your people will be my people, and your God will be my God.

Ruth 1:16

Labouring

In Naomi's home town of Bethlehem, Ruth has no choice but to go gleaning in the harvest fields. The farmer named Boaz is full of admiration for the young foreign woman who is working so hard to provide for Naomi. He is clearly happy to let her take the gleanings from his field, and in doing so he is obeying God's laws.

Early Egyptian tools used in harvesting for cutting the corn. They are not dissimilar to those that the people of Bible times would have used.

Below: Leviticus 23:22 clearly expresses God's laws on gleaning: "When you harvest your fields, do not cut the grain at the edges of the fields… leave them for poor people and foreigners." As a foreigner, Ruth would therefore have been rightly entitled to collect the leftovers. Today, gleaning still continues in some parts of the world, such as Syria.

Gleaning

Farmers allowed poor people to gather up leftover crops from farmers' fields after the harvest. Some ancient cultures saw gleaning as a way of helping the poor, widows, or orphans obtain food.

On the birth of Obed, there was much rejoicing and celebration.

A marriage

Boaz also falls in love with Ruth. He is careful to follow all the local customs and so have the approval of everyone when he marries her. Naomi is delighted to have a family again and especially so when a son is born.

This son, Obed, becomes the grandfather of King David.

Matthew 2:6;
Micah 5:2

Bethlehem

The main scene of the story of Ruth is set in Bethlehem, a place of great significance: it was the birthplace of King David and the town in which he was later anointed as king (see box, page 29) by Samuel (1 Samuel 16:4–13). Bethlehem became known as the "City of David" and was identified as the birthplace of Jesus: "Bethlehem in the land of Judah, you are by no means the least of the leading cities of Judah; for from you will come a leader who will guide my people Israel".

Women continue to harvest wheat outside Bethlehem to this day.

1 SAMUEL

This book is named after the greatest of all the judges: Samuel.

His birth was an answer to prayer for his mother, Hannah. She had promised God that if she had a child, she would dedicate him to God's service.

God calls Samuel

That is how the boy Samuel came to be a helper for the priest, Eli, at a shrine in Shiloh. The old tabernacle stood there, and one of Samuel's jobs was to keep the lamps burning on the lampstand. It was there that he heard God calling him.

Prophet

Samuel is considered to be a prophet; a prophet was God's spokesperson, interpreting Israel's behaviour according to God's laws.

The importance of the Law

God's message to Samuel was that Eli's sons did not live obedient lives and would not be priests after him. They allowed the precious ark of the covenant that contained the tablets of the Law to be led into a battle against the Philistines. They thought the presence of the ark would guarantee victory. But they failed to see that it was obedience to the Law that mattered to God. The two were killed in the fighting and the ark was captured. Eli died when he heard the news.

The Philistines did not benefit from having the ark in their midst. One disaster followed another. Fearful of what might happen next they sent it back to the Israelites on a cart. Its journey ended at a house in a place named Kiriath Jearim, and there it stayed for many years, until the reign of King David (see 1 Chronicles 13:6 and 2 Samuel 6:2–3).

Samuel became the next leader of the people. He insisted that people give up the worship of Baal and Astarte and worship their own God sincerely.

Left: The lamps that Eli and Samuel tended would have looked something like the menorah shown in this picture.

Below: The boy Samuel praying.

The people ask for a king

When Samuel grew old, the people began to worry about who would lead them next. "We want a king," they told Samuel, "so that we will be like other nations" (1 Samuel 8:19–20).

1 Samuel 9:16; 10:1;
1 Kings 1:34, 39; 19:16

Anointing

Each new king would be anointed at a ceremony, with the new king having special oil poured over his head. It was a symbolic act that showed that God was helping the king to carry out his duty.

Saul: Israel's first king

God told Samuel to choose a young man named Saul, and to anoint him: the ceremony of pouring oil over his head was a sign of God having chosen him.

Saul proved to be a brave warrior, but his trust in God wavered. He found it equally hard to trust the advice of Samuel, even though he knew that Samuel was God's prophet.

As a result, Samuel lost faith in Saul. God told Samuel to anoint another: a shepherd boy named David, who is the son of Jesse and the grandson of Obed (see 1 Samuel 15, 16, and Ruth, pages 26–27).

David: Israel's second king

In an important battle against the Philistines, a young man named David killed the giant Goliath and became the people's hero. Saul became so jealous of David that the young man had to flee for his life. For many years he lived as an outlaw. Even so, he never challenged Saul nor tried to claim the throne.

Then, when Samuel died, Saul was in despair. He had no one to advise him any more. In another battle against the Philistines, both he and his son Jonathan were killed.

David's only weapon with which he slayed the mighty giant Goliath was a slingshot and five rounded, smooth stones. He would have learnt to use these defending his sheep against wild animals.

2 SAMUEL

The second book of Samuel continues the story of 1 Samuel. David is overcome with grief at the death of Saul and Jonathan, but he also knows that the time has come for him to claim the kingdom. He overcomes all rivals within the nation and also wins an important victory over the Philistines.

A new city

David sets about establishing his kingdom with great determination. It is a hard struggle to win support for his claim to be king. As he does so, he decides to capture a hill fort named Jebus. He wants to make it the site of his new capital city: Jerusalem. It will be a clear sign of his power.

David is also enthusiastic in his faith. He wants the worship of God to be in the city. He has the tabernacle set up there and arranges for the ark of the covenant to be brought to the city.

He then consults a prophet named Nathan: how could it be right, he asked, for him to be living in a palace while the place of worship was just a tent? God's message to David is that it is not he who will build a temple, but one of his sons. Even so, God makes David a promise: "You will always have descendants, and I will make your kingdom last forever" (2 Samuel 7:16).

David goes on to defeat all his nation's enemies. His personal life, however, is greatly flawed.

Left: Map shows how David's new city of Jerusalem would have looked at the time.

Right: Pilgrims in the city of Shiloh. Shiloh was the focus of worship from the time of Joshua to the time of Samuel. In the background is the tabernacle (see page 16), which was where God was worshipped until the Temple in Jerusalem was built by King Solomon.

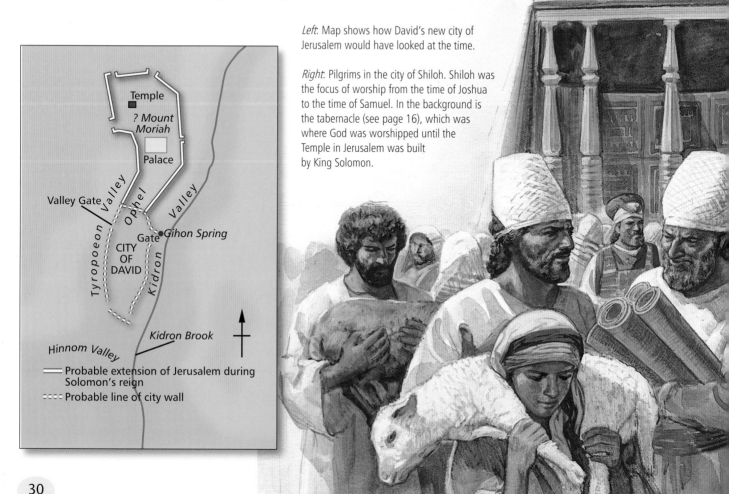

Temple
? Mount Moriah
Palace
Tyropoeon Valley
Ophel
Valley Gate
Kidron Valley
Gate
Gihon Spring
CITY OF DAVID
Kidron Brook
Hinnom Valley

Probable extension of Jerusalem during Solomon's reign
Probable line of city wall

Bathsheba

David falls in love with a woman named Bathsheba, who is the wife of one of his best generals, Uriah. David sends him to a certain death in battle so he can make Bathsheba his wife.

Repentance

The prophet Nathan forces David to admit his wrongdoing in taking another man's wife for his own. Psalm 51, in the book of Psalms, is David's prayer of repentance:

> *Be merciful to me, O God,*
> *because of your constant love.*
> *Because of your great mercy*
> *wipe away my sins!*
>
> *I recognize my faults;*
> *I am always conscious of my sins.*
> *I have sinned against you*
> *– only against you –*
> *and done what you consider evil.*

Psalm 51:1, 3–4

An everlasting kingdom

In spite of his many failings, the stories of David's deeds show that he always puts his trust in God and firmly believes that God has protected him.

His final words reveal his complete confidence that his descendants will rule an everlasting kingdom.

Absalom

David manages to rule a nation, but he does not take control of the quarrelling among his sons. His third son Absalom leads a rebellion against him and nearly succeeds.

David loses some respect as a result of this episode. He has to work hard to stop enemies among his circle rebelling against him.

> *The God of Israel has spoken;*
> *the protector of Israel said to me:*
> *"The king who rules with justice,*
> *who rules in obedience to God,*
> *is like the sun shining on a cloudless dawn,*
> *the sun that makes the grass sparkle after rain."*
>
> *And that is how God will bless my descendants,*
> *because he has made an eternal covenant with me,*
> *an agreement that will not be broken,*
> *a promise that will not be changed.*

2 Samuel 23:3–5

1 KINGS (1–11)

In the Bible, the book of Kings is divided into two parts, known as 1 Kings and 2 Kings. They are in fact a whole and together they describe the history of the people of Israel from the end of the reign of King David, around 970 BCE, to the time when the Babylonian army destroyed Jerusalem and the Jewish people were exiled in around 586 BCE.

These two books were probably written toward the end of this period. They draw on information that had been kept in official records and they give an interpretation of why things worked out the way they did.

The main theme is clear: when the nation and its ruler are obedient to God, they enjoy God's blessing. But when the nation and its ruler are disobedient, God allows the nation's enemies to defeat them.

Chapters 1–11 describe the reign of the king who ruled after David: Solomon, the son of David and Bathsheba.

The judgment of Solomon

When Solomon was a young man he asked God for wisdom and ruled well. The book records him judging between two women. They came to him each claiming to be the mother of a baby. Solomon listened to their pleas and declared that the baby be cut in half. One woman begged for the other to have it whole. He gave the child to the woman who pleaded for its life. "She is the real mother," he said (see 1 Kings 3:16–28).

Solomon attempts to decide to which woman the baby belongs.

For Solomon's Temple, no expense was spared (his vast wealth is described in 2 Chronicles 9:13–29). It was a huge project, for which 3,300 officials were employed, and the detailed descriptions of the building can be read about in 1 Kings 6–7 and 2 Chronicles 3–4. Laid out in the same way as the tabernacle, the Temple was later destroyed (in 586 BCE), when the Babylonians invaded Jerusalem.

Solomon's Temple

Solomon arranged for the building of a spectacular Temple. This project was the completion of a plan his father, David, had made, and the design was based on that of the tabernacle. It was finely crafted from the very best materials over a period of seven years. From the outside its stone gleamed white and the entrance columns were bronze. The doors and the interior were covered in gold. When it was completed, the ark of the covenant was brought into its innermost room, the Holy of Holies (see Leviticus 16:2–34).

At the ceremony of dedication, Solomon prayed these words:

Watch over this Temple day and night, this place where you have chosen to be worshipped. Hear me when I face this Temple and pray. Hear my prayers and the prayers of your people when they face this place and pray. In your home in heaven hear us and forgive us.

1 Kings 8:29–30

King Solomon also reminded the people to keep God's laws. The kingdom prospered, and Solomon became famous. The queen of Sheba heard of Solomon's wealth and wisdom and came from far away to visit. She was most impressed with what she saw (see chapter 10:1–9).

Solomon's disobedience

However, as Solomon grew older he came to love luxury more than wisdom. He forgot to obey God's laws. The people he ruled were forced to pay high taxes and also to work on his grand building projects.

When he died, the people he ruled were eager for change.

See Proverbs, Ecclesiastes, Song of Songs. These books of wisdom belong to the time of Solomon. They may have been written, at least in part, by King Solomon himself.

King Solomon was keen to develop and expand the trade routes on land and on sea, thanks to an impressive fleet of international ships being at his disposal. This map shows the extent of Solomon's empire, and the trade routes into and out of it.

1. Horses from Kue

2. Hiram of Tyre supplied cedar for building projects

3. Horses and chariots exported to the Hittites and Syrians

4. Horses and chariots imported from Egypt

5. Copper from mines near Ezion Geber

6. The queen of Sheba brought spices, gold and jewels (1 Kings 10)

7. Red Sea fleet traded copper from Ezion Geber and gold from Ophir, along with hardwood, silver, ivory, and jewels

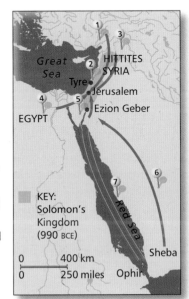

1 KINGS (12–22)

When Solomon died, the tribes in the north of the kingdom asked his son Rehoboam to treat them better. He refused, and the tribes rebelled (1 Kings 12:1–20).

The divided kingdom

The kingdom split into two: a man named Jeroboam claimed the throne of a new northern kingdom named Israel. Rehoboam remained king of a smaller kingdom, Judah, to the south.

Jeroboam did not want his people going to Judah to worship at the Temple. Instead he built new places of worship at Bethel and Dan, each with a golden calf to represent God (1 Kings 12:29). The book of Kings notes this as a sign of fatal disobedience (verse 30).

Kings good and bad

From this point on in the books of Kings many rulers are dealt with in just a few lines: typically they say how and when they came to power, one or two events of their reign, and how and when they died (see 2 Kings 15:7, 23 and 2 Kings 16:14, 20). Everything else the kings did is recorded in *The History of the Kings of Judah* or *The History of the Kings of Israel* as appropriate. These other books are not part of the Bible.

The kings of Israel are generally dismissed as being unfaithful to God. In Judah, some kings do remain true to their faith.

Ahab, Jezebel, and Elijah

There is one king of Israel in particular – Ahab – who is held up as an example of faithlessness. The path of his wrongdoing is clear. He marries a foreign princess, Jezebel, and even builds a temple for her god Baal in his kingdom.

Only one prophet of God dares challenge him. Elijah. He warns Ahab that his kingdom is going to be punished by a severe drought. Elijah goes into hiding for the three years it lasts and returns to challenge the prophets of Baal to a contest on Mount Carmel (1 Kings 18:16–46). Can they light the offering on an altar simply by appealing to their god? They try for hours, and fail, in spite of frenzied rituals.

This map shows how the kingdom was split into the Northern Kingdom (Israel) and the Southern Kingdom (Judah).

Then Elijah orders the altar to be drenched. When everything is soaking wet he prays to God. By a miracle, the altar is set alight.

After that, the drought ends in a tremendous storm. Elijah once again has to flee. Jezebel is furious at the way her prophets have been shamed and vows revenge.

An ivory tablet depicting a "woman in the window", a popular Phoenician theme possibly connected with the goddess Astarte. It is evocative of Jezebel, on the day of Jehu's coup, looking out of the palace window as Jehu approaches (2 Kings 9:30).

Elijah and Jehu

Elijah flees to the wilderness. There God tells him to anoint Hazael king of Syria and a young officer named Jehu king of Israel. This is a clear threat: Elijah is choosing the man who will end the rule of Ahab's family.

Ahab, Jezebel, and Naboth

Then Ahab makes another huge mistake. He wants to buy the vineyard of a man named Naboth so he can extend his own garden. Naboth refuses to sell.

Queen Jezebel has Naboth accused on made-up charges and condemned to death. Then she tells Ahab he can go and claim the vineyard (1 Kings 21:1–29).

Elijah returns to tell Ahab that God will not allow his family to rule the kingdom after his death. Not long after, Ahab dies in battle, shot by an arrow as he watches the fighting from his chariot (1 Kings 22:34–37).

Elijah calls down the fire from heaven.

35

2 KINGS

Elijah continued to speak on behalf of God to the king who came after Ahab. Then, knowing his time had come, he chose Elisha to be a prophet after him (2 Kings 2).

Elisha

Elisha became feared and respected for his miracles. He even cured a foreigner – Naaman the Syrian – by simply telling him to bathe in the River Jordan that flowed through Israel (2 Kings 5).

In time Elisha became the person who prompted the overthrow of Ahab's family line: God told him to go to the young army officer named Jehu whom Elijah had anointed king and perform another ceremony of anointing.

In a panel from the Black Obelisk of King Shalmaneser III, c. 825 BCE, Jehu, the king of Israel (on his knees), offers King Shalmaneser III tributes, including silver and gold.

Below. Namaan, a commander of the king's army in Syria, was afflicted by leprosy, a skin disease. Elisha advised him to wash seven times in the River Jordan. Having been cured, he then praised God.

Jehu

Jehu accepted the challenge. When he drove his chariot to the palace in the city of Jezreel to claim the throne, even the palace servants went over to his side.

In the early days Jehu tried to make the nation worship God as they should, but, says 2 Kings, he did not obey the law with all his heart (10:31). The nation soon found itself being threatened by a powerful enemy to the north. Jehu had to send tribute gifts to avoid defeat in battle.

Books in parallel

Hosea and Amos

Two prophets were outspoken in their warnings to people in the kingdom of Israel during the reign of King Jeroboam II described in 2 Kings 14. Both Amos and Hosea rail against the godlessness of the people.

Hosea 1:2;
Amos 2:4

Jonah

The story of Jonah is set in a period when the Assyrians in their capital city of Nineveh are regarded as the wickedest nation of all.

Jonah 1:2

The defeat of Israel

In chapter 17, the kings that came after Jehu were no more faithful to God than any of the kings before had been. As long as they paid tribute they were allowed to stay in power. However, when one named Hoshea decided to stop buying peace in this way, the Assyrian king Shalmaneser V attacked. Israel was defeated and its people sent to live in other parts of the Assyrian empire. Other defeated people were brought into Israel to make it their home.

Referenced in 2 Kings 18, during the reign of King Hezekiah of Judah, in 701 BCE, the Jewish town of Lachish (about 30 miles from Jerusalem) was attacked by the Assyrian king Sennacherib. In this relief from Sennacherib's palace in Nineveh, flaming torches are thrown from the wall by the defenders.

KINGS & PROPHETS OF THE OLD TESTAMENT

The chart below sets kings, queens, and prophets within their historical setting. Note that the prophets' dates relate to the period during which they were speaking, rather than the dates the books were written.

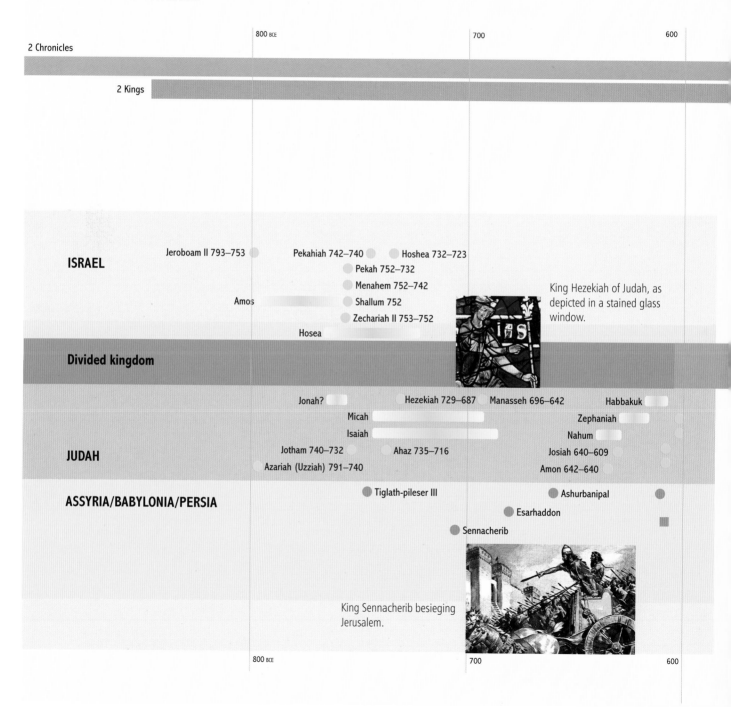

	800 BCE	700	600
2 Chronicles			
2 Kings			

ISRAEL

Jeroboam II 793–753 Pekahiah 742–740 Hoshea 732–723
Pekah 752–732
Menahem 752–742
Amos Shallum 752
Zechariah II 753–752
Hosea

Divided kingdom

King Hezekiah of Judah, as depicted in a stained glass window.

Jonah? Hezekiah 729–687 Manasseh 696–642 Habbakuk
Micah Zephaniah
Isaiah Nahum

JUDAH

Jotham 740–732 Ahaz 735–716 Josiah 640–609
Azariah (Uzziah) 791–740 Amon 642–640

ASSYRIA/BABYLONIA/PERSIA

Tiglath-pileser III Ashurbanipal
Esarhaddon
Sennacherib

King Sennacherib besieging Jerusalem.

	800 BCE	700	600

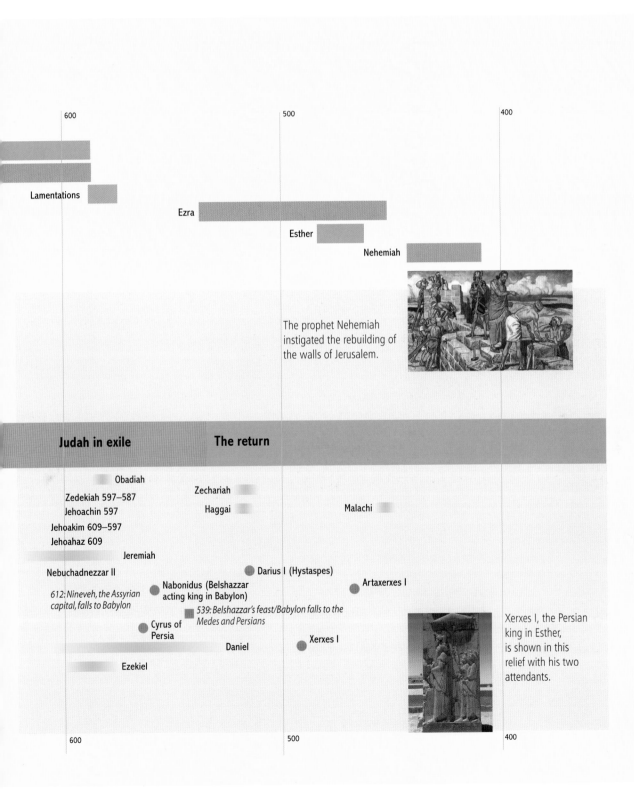

600

500

400

Lamentations

Ezra

Esther

Nehemiah

The prophet Nehemiah instigated the rebuilding of the walls of Jerusalem.

Judah in exile

The return

Obadiah

Zedekiah 597–587

Zechariah

Jehoachin 597

Haggai

Malachi

Jehoakim 609–597

Jehoahaz 609

Jeremiah

Nebuchadnezzar II

Darius I (Hystaspes)

Nabonidus (Belshazzar acting king in Babylon)

Artaxerxes I

612: Nineveh, the Assyrian capital, falls to Babylon

539: Belshazzar's feast/Babylon falls to the Medes and Persians

Cyrus of Persia

Xerxes I

Daniel

Xerxes I

Ezekiel

Xerxes I, the Persian king in Esther, is shown in this relief with his two attendants.

600

500

400

2 KINGS (1–20)

The books of Kings note the successive reigns of the kings of Judah in parallel with those of the kings of Israel. It is clear that obedience to God is linked with success, and disobedience with failure and defeat.

Judah's rulers are a mixture of good and bad

In the same year that Jehu becomes king of Israel, a woman named Athaliah seizes the throne and rules as queen – the only queen to rule in her own right in the entire history of the kings of Israel and Judah.

She was the daughter of Israel's king Ahab, and she seized power when her son, King Ahaziah of Judah, was killed in battle (2 Kings 8:26). She is overthrown in favour of her grandson with the same cruelty she herself demonstrated when she took the throne (2 Kings 11:1–16).

During the reign of King Hezekiah, Jerusalem was threatened by an Assyrian attack. Seven years earlier Assyria had destroyed the kingdom of Israel; now it was Judah's turn.

Books in parallel

Isaiah and Micah

Isaiah and Micah were two prophets who lived during the reigns of the kings of Judah in the eighth century BCE.

Isaiah 37:14–20

Chapters 1–39 of the book of the prophet Isaiah are addressed to the kingdom of Judah in the years leading up to and including the reign of King Hezekiah.

Jerusalem is saved when some disaster causes death to ravage the Assyrian camp. This is seen as a miracle – God has sent the angel of death (37:36).

Micah

The prophet Micah gives his message at the time when Samaria in the kingdom of Israel is facing defeat and Jerusalem is threatened.

A second panel from Lachish shows the Assyrian army carrying away the spoils of war as well as captives.

King Hezekiah

At the time that King Shalmaneser overruns Israel, Judah is ruled by King Hezekiah. When Sennacherib becomes king, his army defeats the cities of Judah and lays siege to Jerusalem.

Hezekiah is frantic. Luckily, he has a wise prophet named Isaiah, who gives him reassurance: Hezekiah cannot defeat the enemy, but God can (2 Kings 18–19).

An impression of how King Hezekiah, seated on his throne, may have dictated a letter through a scribe to King Sennacherib, who was in Lachish (see pages 36–37 and 2 Kings 18:13–14).

2 KINGS (21–25)

These final chapters of the second book of Kings cover the hundred years between the end of King Hezekiah's reign around 686 BCE and the final destruction of Jerusalem and its Temple in 586 BCE.

Two bad kings, Manasseh and Amon, are succeeded by a boy king, Josiah. Worship of the gods of other nations is rife.

Josiah: The golden era

Josiah is a remarkable king who is faithful to God and God's laws. As a young man he makes arrangements for repairs to the Temple to be carried out in a fair and proper manner. During the work a book of the Law is discovered. Josiah has it read aloud and is dismayed to discover the number of laws that have been forgotten. He orders his people to turn away from worshipping false gods and he arranges for the nation to celebrate the festival of Passover (2 Kings 22, 23). The years 640–609 BCE are a golden period.

> *There had never been a king like him before, who served the Lord with all his heart, mind, and strength, obeying all the Law of Moses; nor has there been a king like him since.*

2 Kings 23:25

A succession of kings

However, by the end of Josiah's reign the king of Egypt has begun a war against Judah to support the Assyrians. The next king, Joahaz, dies in battle. After him comes Jehoiakim. During his reign King Nebuchadnezzar of Babylon becomes the major threat to Judah, eclipsing the threat from Assyria. Jehoiakim is forced to pay heavily to avoid invasion (2 Kings 23).

King Josiah reads the book of the Law, which reminds people of the time when Moses led the people out of slavery. A passion for worshipping God is rediscovered.

Jehoiachin

After Jehoiakim comes Jehoiachin. King Nebuchadnezzar's armies come and lay siege to Jerusalem. They carry off the Temple treasures and deport many of the most educated official skilled workers to live in exile in Babylon. Even the king is taken into exile (chapter 24).

Zedekiah

The final king, Zedekiah, is the puppet of King Nebuchadnezzar. Zedekiah tries to rebel against him. The result is that the Babylonians conduct a major offensive on Jerusalem. The city and the Temple are destroyed in 586 BCE (2 Kings 25).

This clay tablet, part of the Babylonian Chronicle, records some of the events of King Nebuchadnezzar's Babylonian empire from 605 to 594 BCE, including the capture of Jerusalem in 597 BCE.

Prophets at the time

Below are the books of those prophets who spoke out at the time of the kings listed in 2 Kings 21–25.

Zephaniah

The book of Zephaniah denounces worship of false gods in the period before the reforms of King Josiah.

Nahum

The book of Nahum rejoices over the fall of the Assyrian capital city of Nineveh.

Habakkuk

The book of Habakkuk complains to God of the new threat to the nation of Judah from the Babylonians.

Jeremiah

The prophet Jeremiah speaks to the nation of Judah on behalf of God from 627 BCE, during the reign of King Josiah to the end. His words provide a commentary on the faithlessness of the final kings and the refusal of the nation to live as God's people.

Lamentations

The book of Lamentations describes the horrors of life in the city of Jerusalem that had been defeated by the Babylonians.

Obadiah

The book of Obadiah criticizes another nation, the Edomites, for gloating over the destruction of Jerusalem.

1 & 2 CHRONICLES

The books named Chronicles are a carefully composed history of the Jewish people. Many experts think that the author of this work is Ezra, a priest who was a key figure in the reestablishment of the nation after years in exile (see pages 46–47).

The author has clearly researched other writings to put together this history. Much of Chronicles is drawn from the books of Samuel and Kings. The material is chosen to give a particular slant on history: that God is taking care of his people, in spite of the many disasters that they have endured.

1 Chronicles

The first book of Chronicles begins with the family tree of the nation, starting from the very beginning, with Adam, and including King David. It describes how David made Jerusalem his capital city, brought the covenant box there, and made plans to build a Temple.

2 Chronicles

The second book of Chronicles describes the building of the Temple during the reign of King Solomon (see also page 33). This moment of celebration is followed by an account of the troubled years after King Solomon's reign, when the kingdom was divided. Israel's rulers are faithless and eventually the kingdom is defeated and destroyed. Many of the rulers of Judah are also wicked and faithless, but some strive to keep the Law and make sure that God is worshipped in the Temple – Hezekiah and Josiah among them.

Destruction and exile

The kings after them are not faithful to God. They do not listen to the prophets. It is God who brings King Nebuchadnezzar of Babylon to punish the nation. Jerusalem and the Temple are destroyed. The people are taken into exile in Babylon where they live for seventy years. It is in this period that they become known as the Jews.

Then King Cyrus of Persia becomes the ruler of the old Babylonian empire. He allows the Jewish exiles to return (2 Chronicles 36:23).

There they must rebuild their Temple. It is a new beginning for God's own people.

Left: In exile the Jewish people were exposed to the religion and culture of the Babylonians, including their festivals, celebrations, and Akkadian stories. But they remained steadfast in their faith in God.

Below: The clay Cyrus cylinder gives a Babylonian account of the conquest of Babylon by King Cyrus in 539 BCE and includes a decree allowing the Jews to return to Judah to rebuild the temple. The text shows that the cylinder was written to be buried in the foundations of the city wall of Babylon after it had been captured.

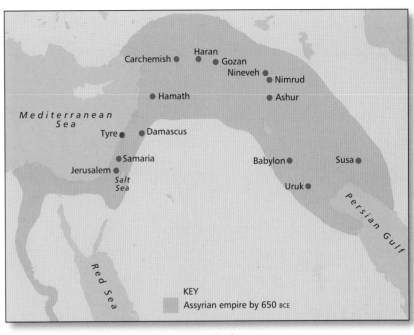

Map showing the expanse of the Assyrian empire by the time of 650 BCE. The empire was then taken by Babylon, destroying Jerusalem and conquering Judah.

Other books in the Bible concerned with the exile

Isaiah
Chapters 40–55 of the book of the prophet Isaiah are addressed to the exiles in Babylon.

Ezekiel
The prophet Ezekiel speaks to the people of Judah who were taken to live in Babylon.

Daniel
The book of Daniel tells remarkable stories of God's protection for those who are faithful. The stories describe the cruelties of Babylonian kings and the Persian rulers who overcame them.

Psalms 73–89 and 90–106
These groups of psalms belong to the time of the exile.

EZRA

The books of Ezra and Nehemiah give an account of the resettling of Jerusalem years after it was destroyed by King Nebuchadnezzar of Babylon in 586 BCE.

In 539 BCE the Persian emperor Cyrus issued a decree allowing the various nations who lived in exile to return to their homeland. A small group of Jews set out for Jerusalem.

The Temple (Ezra 3–6)

It was not just about making their home there. They wanted to rebuild the Temple so they could worship God in the way they believed to be right.

However, the land had not been empty while they were away. Other peoples had made their homes there, and they objected to the rebuilding of the Temple. The work was stopped.

A few years later, two prophets, Haggai (Haggai 1:2–11) and Zechariah (Zechariah 1:16) urged the people to be bolder. It was God's plan that they rebuild the Temple (Ezra 5:1).

Ezra the scholar

In 458 BCE Ezra is chosen to go to Jerusalem to teach the people how to live and worship.

> *Ezra had devoted his life to studying the Law of the Lord, to practising it, and to teaching all its laws and regulations to the people of Israel.*
> **Ezra 7:10**

Ezra was strict in his teaching: for example, he insisted that Jewish men who had married foreign women should divorce them so as to avoid pagan influence in the community (Ezra 10:10–11).

Books in parallel

Haggai and Zechariah

The words of the two prophets who urged the continuation of work on the Temple are also in the Bible.

The Jews sent an appeal to the new Persian emperor Darius, who agreed that they did have the right to rebuild the Temple. The work was done.

Jonah

The book of Jonah provides a question mark against the strict teaching of Ezra. The story shows that God can forgive and accept even the wickedest nation.

Just like Ezra, scribes today copy the Scriptures meticulously.

A new identity

It was in this period that the Jewish people gained a new sense of identity: as a people who were different from others, who obeyed a higher set of laws than others. As the years went by it became necessary for communities to have teachers – rabbis – who would guide them in understanding the ancient writings of their people, the Scriptures.

NEHEMIAH

Nehemiah played a leading role in the rebuilding of Jerusalem. He twice became its governor.

News from Jerusalem

Nearly a hundred years after the first exiles returned to Jerusalem, Nehemiah heard the upsetting news: the city was still not rebuilt and the community was struggling to make a living. At the time Nehemiah had an important job as cupbearer to the Persian king Artaxerxes. He asked for permission to go and help his people, and it was granted (Nehemiah 13:6).

Books in parallel

Isaiah	Malachi	Joel	Psalms 107–150
Chapters 40–55 of the book of the prophet Isaiah are addressed to the exiles in Babylon.	The book of Malachi is written to admonish the priests and people to live and worship as God requires.	No one is quite sure where the prophecy of Joel fits into the pattern of history. Many think it is linked with this period.	This section of the book of Psalms belongs to the time of Ezra.

A programme of rebuilding

Shortly after he arrived, Nehemiah rode around the outside of the city. He was dismayed to see how little progress had been made building a city wall. Quickly he set about organizing a proper rebuilding programme (Nehemiah 2–6).

This didn't just mean building walls: it meant fending off attacks and sabotage from non-Jews who didn't want a city wall.

Soon everything was complete. Nehemiah's practical work and Ezra's religious leadership made a big difference. Together they inspired the Jews who lived in Jerusalem to be faithful to their laws and their traditions (Ezra 8).

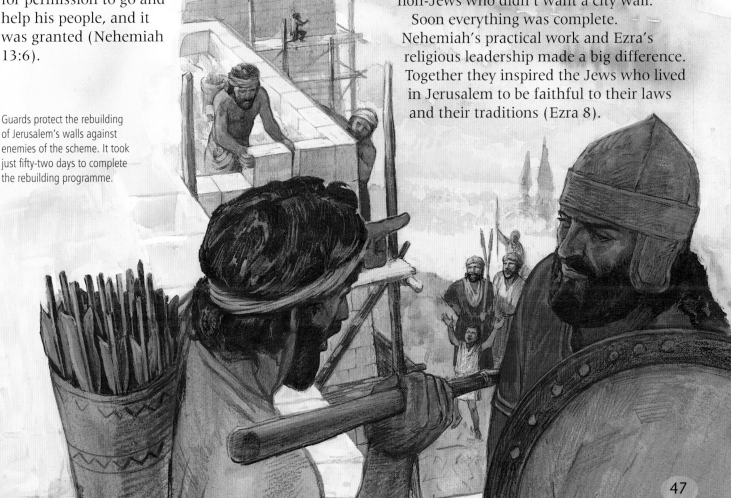

Guards protect the rebuilding of Jerusalem's walls against enemies of the scheme. It took just fifty-two days to complete the rebuilding programme.

ESTHER

The book of Esther tells a story set in the Persian empire. It concerns events in the Persian royal court, and is usually linked to the reign of King Xerxes, who ruled 486–465 BCE. At this time, some Jews had returned to their homeland around Jerusalem. However, there were groups of Jews living freely throughout the empire.

Royal celebrations

The story begins with a day of royal celebration. However, King Xerxes' generous mood ends when his queen, Vashti, refuses to obey him. He arranges for his officials to search the empire for a woman to be his new queen.

A beautiful girl named Esther is chosen. She is Jewish and has been raised by her cousin Mordecai. He himself has worked for the Persian king and even uncovered a plot against his life.

Even so, he warns, Jews are all too often looked down upon. He advises Esther not to let anyone know about her background.

Haman's wicked plot

The king also chooses a second in command: a man named Haman. Haman takes a violent dislike to Mordecai because Mordecai will not bow down to him. He makes a plan to hang Mordecai and orders a massacre of all Jews everywhere.

Mordecai sends a message to Esther. Only she can do anything to stop Haman.

Esther knows she cannot count on the king's support. She is supposed to wait to be summoned – and he hasn't asked to see her for some time.

Bravely she dresses in her finery and approaches the throne. Happily, the king welcomes her. She invites Xerxes and Haman to a banquet. The evening goes well, so she asks them to come a second time.

Where is God?

Esther is the only book of the Bible that does not mention God. However, it demonstrates a key promise from the Bible: that God will take care of his faithful people and protect them from their enemies.

A stone relief depicting the Persian king Xerxes I, son of Darius I.

Before the second banquet, the king has a sleepless night. He asks for the record of his reign to be read aloud to him and is reminded of how Mordecai saved his life.

"I want you to arrange a parade to honour him in public," he tells Haman. "I want it done tomorrow."

Haman has to obey, and is in a bad mood when he arrives for the second banquet. Esther continues to charm the king. When he asks her what favour she would like she seizes the chance to denounce Haman.

The king orders Haman to be hanged on the gallows Haman himself had built for Mordecai, and the Jews are given permission to defend themselves in any attempted massacre. In this way they are able to get rid of their enemies.

Mordecai takes on an important role in government and uses his influence for good.

Above: Darius I built a magnificent palace at Susa, an important Persian city. The walls were decorated with many pictures, including archers in ceremonial dress.

A hoard of precious golden treasure, known as the Oxus Treasure, includes this griffin-headed armlet from the Persian court.

JOB

Often referred to as "wisdom literature", the books listed on the right wrestle with the idea of what it means to be human and how to live well. They give practical advice for living. The majority of these books contain poetry.

The book of Job is something of a mystery. The story it tells is of a wealthy man who possibly lives as a nomad (1:3). This seems to put it in the same era as the great men of Genesis (Genesis 12:4–7; 13:5–12). Nobody really knows when or where it was first told, but it seems likely that it was first written down in the time of King Solomon.

Poetry and wisdom

JOB

PSALMS

PROVERBS

ECCLESIASTES

SONG OF SONGS

One of the disasters that struck Job was the affliction of painful sores all over his body.

Satan let loose

In the story, God and Satan have a conversation. God is pleased to see that Job is unfailingly good in all he does. Satan says he can change that: he can turn Job into someone angry enough to curse God himself.

Satan is allowed to have a go and test Job. Suddenly disasters strike Job. Within the space of a day, Job's wealth, his children, and all his household are destroyed. But Job does not fall into the trap of blaming God for what has happened. However, when three friends come to comfort him he breaks his silence.

"Why did all of this have to happen?" he laments.

False friends

The so-called friends – Eliphaz, Bildad and Zophar – try to make sense of it all, but they all believe the same thing: God must be punishing Job for something wicked.

Job will not cave in. He knows he has always done what is right, and in the past people respected him for it.

God knows everything I do;
he sees every step I take.

I swear I have never acted wickedly
and never tried to deceive others.

Job 31:4–5

The young man's point of view

A younger man, Elihu, joins the conversation.
He has a different point of view. God may allow
people to suffer so that they learn something
valuable from the experience. It may make them
better people.

In any case, explains Elihu, what right has a
mere human being to object to what the God of
the universe does?

Remember how great is God's power;
* he is the greatest teacher of all.*
No one can tell God what to do
* or accuse him of doing evil.*
He has always been praised for what he does;
* you also must praise him.*

Job 36:22–24

Finally, God speaks to Job. God asks him to look
at the world around that God alone has made:
the stars, the oceans, the hills and mountains,
the great variety of living things.

At last Job understands the greatness, and is
sorry for having doubted God's goodness.

So I am ashamed of all I have said
* and repent in dust and ashes.*

Job 42:6

The story has a happy ending: God blesses
Job with more than he had before – he has
wealth, children, grandchildren, and great-
grandchildren.

Despite all the suffering that he endured, Job was able to see
God's glory and greatness. Once again he sees in glorious
technicolour all the wonders of God's creation.

PSALMS 1–106

The book of Psalms is a collection of hymns and prayers, written as poems. They were used by the people of Israel in their worship, from the time of the first Temple to the time of Jesus and beyond.

They cover a wide range of topics: praising God, thanking God, asking for help, asking for guidance among them.

There are 150 psalms that are arranged in five sections dating from different periods.

Psalms 1 to 41

Psalms 1 to 41 were probably collected in the time of King David. The most famous in the section is probably Psalm 23, which reflects David's experience first as a shepherd boy, and later as a fighter leader who needed to put his trust in God.

The Lord is my shepherd;
I have everything I need.
He lets me rest in fields of green grass
and leads me to quiet pools of fresh water.
He gives me new strength.
He guides me in the right paths,
as he has promised.
Even if I go through the deepest darkness,
I will not be afraid, Lord,
for you are with me.
Your shepherd's rod and staff protect me.

You prepare a banquet for me,
where all my enemies can see me;
you welcome me as an honoured guest
and fill my cup to the brim.
I know that your goodness and love will be with
me all my life;
and your house will be my home as long as I
live.

Psalm 23

A total of 73 of the psalms are said to have been written by King David.

An impression of David as a young shepherd boy, looking after sheep and goats.

Psalms 42 to 72

The second section, Psalms 42 to 72, was probably added in the time of King Solomon. Psalm 51 is said to be a Psalm of David. He admits his deep sorrow at some wrongdoing. This is usually said to be his scheming to have a brave soldier Uriah killed so he could make Uriah's wife, Bathsheba, his own (2 Samuel 11).

Be merciful to me, O God,
  because of your constant love.
Because of your great mercy
  wipe away my sins!
Wash away all my evil
  and make me clean from my sin!

Create a pure heart in me, O God,
  and put a new and loyal spirit in me.

Give me again the joy that comes from your salvation,
  and make me willing to obey you.

51:1–2, 10, 12

In the third and fourth sections of Psalms, the Jewish people lament for the destruction of Jerusalem and feel, at times, hopeless.

Psalms 73 to 89, and 90 to 106

Section 3 includes Psalms 73 to 89, and section 4 from 90 to 106. These psalms were probably collected together at the time of the exile, although many may be much older than that. Some of them talk directly about the longing of the people to return home.

Turn to us, Almighty God!
  Look down from heaven at us;
  come and save your people!
Come and save this grapevine that you planted,
  this young vine you made grow so strong!

  Our enemies have set it on fire and cut it down;
      look at them in anger and destroy them!
    Preserve and protect the people you have chosen,
    the nation you made so strong.
  We will never turn away from you again;
  keep us alive, and we will praise you.

    Bring us back, Lord God Almighty.
      Show us your mercy, and we will be saved.

80:14–19

PSALMS 107–150

The fifth section is a collection of psalms that may have been put together in the time of Ezra.

Words for comfort

During this period, when they were far from Jerusalem and the Temple had been razed, the people looked to their Scriptures to feel close to God. Here, indeed, was treasure that could not be taken from them:

Your word is a lamp to guide me
and a light for my path.
I will keep my solemn promise
to obey your just instructions.

Your commandments are my eternal
possession;
they are the joy of my heart.
I have decided to obey your laws
until the day I die.

119:105–106, 111–112

Some give God thanks for letting the people come home (see pages 46–47).

When the Lord brought us back to Jerusalem,
it was like a dream!
How we laughed, how we sang for joy!
Then the other nations said about us,
"The Lord did great things for them."
Indeed he did great things for us;
how happy we were!

126:1–3

Made from clay, oil lamps, such as that mentioned in Psalm 119:105, have been found in many ancient civilizations.

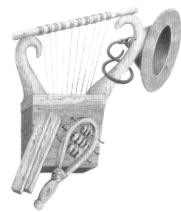
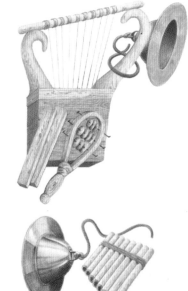

Examples of musical instruments – percussion, pipes and strings – that would have been played during worship in the Temple. The psalms encourage people to praise God with all kinds of instruments.

Lively worship

Worship in the Temple could be a lively affair, as Psalm 150 indicates.

Praise the Lord!

Praise God in his Temple!

Praise him with trumpets.
Praise him with harps and lyres.
Praise him with drums and dancing.
Praise him with harps and flutes.
Praise him with cymbals.
Praise him with loud cymbals.
Praise the Lord, all living creatures!

Praise the Lord!

150:1, 3–6

Music has played an important part in the worship life of many civilizations. Here, musicians play stringed instruments in the court of the Assyrian king Ashurbanipal.

Priests sing psalms and play various instruments outside the Temple.

Matthew 26:30

Psalms 113–118

Psalms 113 and 114 are traditionally sung in Jewish homes before the Passover meal, since they refer to the exodus and deliverance, and Psalms 115–118 are sung after it.

PROVERBS

The book of Proverbs is a collection of short sayings comprising practical wisdom for everyday living. They are thought to be the work of King Solomon (see pages 32–33).

One of the history books (1 Kings 4:29, 32) provides a clue:

God gave Solomon unusual wisdom and insight, and knowledge too great to be measured… He composed three thousand proverbs and more than a thousand songs.

Collected as a book

The book itself states that the proverbs were collected together as a book in the time of King Hezekiah of Judah (Proverbs 25:1) and at the end of the book are other proverbs by Agur (Proverbs 30) and Lemuel (31).

Wisdom for life

The proverbs are not in any particular order and can seem hard to work out. Even so, taken together they advise people to be sober, faithful in marriage, hardworking, humble, generous to those in need, and committed to justice. Those who live in this way will reap the rewards of good living, even though it may seem at times that foolish and arrogant people are making more money and having more fun.

"If you oppress poor people, you insult the God who made them; but kindness shown to the poor is an act of worship" (Proverbs 14:31).

Lazy people should learn a lesson from the way ants live.
6:6

If you stay calm, you are wise, but if you have a hot temper, you only show how stupid you are.
14:29

It is better to have a little, honestly earned, than to have a large income gained dishonestly.
16:8

If you want people to like you, forgive them when they wrong you. Remembering wrongs can break up a friendship.
17:9

Being cheerful keeps you healthy. It is slow death to be gloomy all the time.

17:22

If you spend your time sleeping, you will be poor. Keep busy and you will have plenty to eat.

20:13

Don't be envious of sinful people; let reverence for the Lord be the concern of your life. If it is, you have a bright future.

23:17–18

Stupid people express their anger openly, but sensible people are patient and hold it back.

29:11

Correction and discipline are good for children. If they have their own way, they will make their mothers ashamed of them.

29:15

ECCLESIASTES

Ecclesiastes begins with this statement: "These are the words of the Philosopher, David's son, who was king in Jerusalem."

Many scholars take this to mean that the author is King Solomon himself. It certainly gives the impression of being written by someone who is looking back on their life with a sense of having lost their faith and wanting to have that faith once more.

Life is useless...

The author states that his aim is to use his own power of reasoning to work out what life is all about. What he sees is rather gloomy.

It is useless, useless... Life is useless, all useless. You spend your life working... and what do you have to show for it?... What has happened before will happen again. What has been done before will be done again. There is nothing new in the whole world.

Ecclesiastes 1:2–3, 9

The writer knows what it is to be rich and powerful, and has enjoyed himself. Now he sees that everything he did will come to nothing. He will die like the animals.

He has found out that life is often unfair:

Written in Hebrew, the "Gezer Calendar" lists the seasons of the farmer's year, explaining when each task should be completed. "There is a time for everything, and a season for every activity under the heavens" – so says Ecclesiastes 3:1 (NIV).

I realized another thing, that in this world fast runners do not always win the races, and the brave do not always win the battles. The wise do not always earn a living, intelligent people do not always get rich, and capable people do not always rise to high positions. Bad luck happens to everyone.

Ecclesiastes 9:11

Is it odd to find the book of Ecclesiastes in the Bible? The writer of it seems to be someone who has lost both hope and faith. Perhaps it is included because so many people find themselves feeling just as downcast and despairing sometimes. Anyone can feel this way... and still be one of God's people.

The writer of Ecclesiastes encourages the young to enjoy their lives, but also emphasizes the inevitability of death (11:8–10).

View of God

The writer does believe there is a God, but a God who is too far away for a mere human being to understand. The best a person can do is to enjoy life in a sensible way, staying out of trouble and obeying God's commands.

SONG OF SONGS

This book consists of love poems – between a beautiful young woman and a man who is tall, dark, handsome, and strong. It is quite clear from the verses that they are very attracted to one another.

A puzzle or a celebration?

Over the centuries, people have puzzled about why a book like this is in the Bible. Perhaps it is really about the love God has for his chosen people, or, if we are to think in New Testament terms, the love of Christ for the church.

Then again, it may be simply what it seems to be: a celebration of physical attraction and love. After all, God made human beings to feel that way.

The text of Song of Songs is a popular choice for a reading even in modern-day wedding ceremonies, due to its joyful celebration of love between a bride and her groom.

A wedding

Here a bride and groom are seated under a "chuppah", the name given to a ceremonial wedding canopy. A cloth or sheet is stretched over four poles. It symbolizes the home that the couple will build together.

Psalm 19:5;
Joel 2:16

ISAIAH (1–39)

A prophet was God's spokesperson on earth, chosen to speak to people on God's behalf at various points in Israel's history. Often their messages took the form of a warning; at other times they were messages of hope.

Isaiah was a prophet who lived in Jerusalem in Judah, prophesying for forty years during the reign of four kings: Uzziah, Jotham, Ahaz, and Hezekiah.

Major prophets

- ISAIAH
- JEREMIAH
- LAMENTATIONS
- EZEKIEL
- DANIEL

Enemies of God

The words of the prophet in chapters 1–39 speak before the exile of the threat from enemy peoples, especially Assyria, to the north.

However, the prophet warns, the main threat to the nation is not enemies. God can deal with those. The real threat comes from the fact the people are not faithful to God. They are not living as God's people should.

Such sinfulness will bring disaster, warns the prophet.

A king is foretold

Even so, the time will come when a king like David will defeat the nation's enemies and make them free to be God's people again.

The people who walked in darkness
  have seen a great light.
They lived in a land of shadows,
  but now light is shining on them.

A child is born to us!
  A son is given to us!
  And he will be our ruler.
He will be called, "Wonderful Counsellor,"
  "Mighty God," "Eternal Father,"
  "Prince of Peace."
His royal power will continue to grow;
  his kingdom will always be at peace.
He will rule as King David's successor,
  basing his power on right and justice,
  from now until the end of time.

Isaiah 9:2, 6–7

Isaiah warns the people of Jerusalem about their unjust behaviour.

Isaiah's foretelling of a king like David is understood by Christians to predict the birth of Jesus. The passages from Isaiah 9 are often read aloud in churches at Christmas.

Isaiah foresees a day when there is universal peace, with humankind and wild animals living in harmony without fear of one another.

The royal line of David is like a tree that has been cut down; but just as new branches sprout from a stump, so a new king will arise from among David's descendants.

> *The spirit of the Lord will give him wisdom,*
>   *and the knowledge and skill to rule his*
>   *people.*
> *He will know the Lord's will and honour*
>   *him,*
>   *and find pleasure in obeying him.*
> *He will not judge by appearance or*
>   *hearsay;*
>   *he will judge the poor fairly*
>   *and defend the rights of the helpless.*
>
> *He will rule his people with justice*
>   *and integrity.*

Isaiah 11:1–4, 5

The reign of this great king, says the prophet, will be a time of universal peace when even wild animals will live together.

The Assyrian threat

Chapters 36 to 38 speak of a major event in the reign of King Hezekiah that is also found in the book of Kings (2 Kings 19). The Assyrian army has swept down and crushed the kingdom of Israel. They have invaded Judah and are camped around Jerusalem. King Hezekiah is desperate. Defeat seems close.

By a miracle, the angel of death strikes the Assyrians one night. The disaster causes the emperor, Sennacherib, to abandon the fight and go home.

This prism (known as "Taylor's Prism") records the military expeditions of Sennacherib, the king of Assyria, and in particular his siege against Jerusalem. He says that he locked Hezekiah up "like a bird in a cage" in Jerusalem.

ISAIAH (40–55)

The book that bears the name of the prophet Isaiah has a middle section that talks about a period after the time of the prophet himself. Chapters 40–55 are spoken to the people who have been exiled in Babylon.

God's love and faithfulness

The defeat of Jerusalem was a consequence of the people's faithlessness. Yet God still loves his people and will restore their fortunes.

*The Sovereign Lord is coming
to rule with power,
  bringing with him the people
he has rescued.
He will take care of his flock
like a shepherd;
  he will gather the lambs together
  and carry them in his arms;
  he will gently lead their mothers.*

Isaiah 40:10–11

One day, they will be free again:

*You will leave Babylon with joy;
you will be led out of the city in
peace.
The mountains and hills will burst
into singing,
and the trees will shout for joy.
Cypress trees will grow where now
there are briars;
  myrtle trees will come up in place
  of thorns.*

Isaiah 55:12–13

In several passages, the prophet speaks of God's servant:

*The Lord says,
"My servant will succeed in his task;
  he will be highly honoured. …
It was my will that he should suffer;
his death was a sacrifice to bring
forgiveness. …
After a life of suffering, he will again
have joy;
he will know that he did not suffer in
vain.
My devoted servant, with whom I am
pleased,
will bear the punishment of many
and for his sake I will forgive them."*

Isaiah 52:13; 53:10–11

Above: A cypress tree grows in Jerusalem.

Left: An imaginative depiction of the Babylonian exile.

Suffering servant

Isaiah's descriptions of God's servant who suffers dreadful punishment on behalf of others are treasured by Christians. For them, the suffering servant is Jesus.

In the New Testament, Jesus likens himself to the "Good Shepherd", depicted here in a painting by James Tissot. Jesus is linked to Isaiah 40:10–11: "The Sovereign Lord is coming to rule with power, bringing with him the people he has rescued. He will take care of his flock like a shepherd; he will gather the lambs together and carry them in his arms; he will gently lead their mothers." See also Ezekiel 34:11, 13, 15–16.

ISAIAH (56–65)

The final chapters of Isaiah contain a message for the people who returned to Jerusalem to rebuild the nation.

Living as God wants

The people need to live as God's people should. This means much more than keeping up a show of being religious. It means being kind and fair to all:

Remove the chains of oppression and the yoke of injustice, and let the oppressed go free. Share your food with the hungry and open your homes to the homeless poor. Give clothes to those who have nothing to wear, and do not refuse to help your own relatives.

Isaiah 58:6–7

One day, the prophet says, someone will come who will make all God's promises to his people come true.

The Sovereign Lord has filled me with
*   his Spirit.*
He has chosen me and sent me
To bring good news to the poor,
To heal the broken-hearted,
To announce release to captives
And freedom to those in prison.
He has sent me to proclaim
That the time has come
When the Lord will save his people…

Isaiah 61:1–2

The sharing of food, as shown in this picture, is an example of fair and charitable living.

This passage became part of the treasured Scriptures of the Jewish people as they rebuilt their nation. As such, it was one of many – including others from the book of Isaiah – that would be read aloud at the weekly synagogue meetings.

Map showing how the Jews dispersed across the ancient world after the exiles. The Jewish communities would set up their own meeting places, or synagogues, in the places where they began to settle.

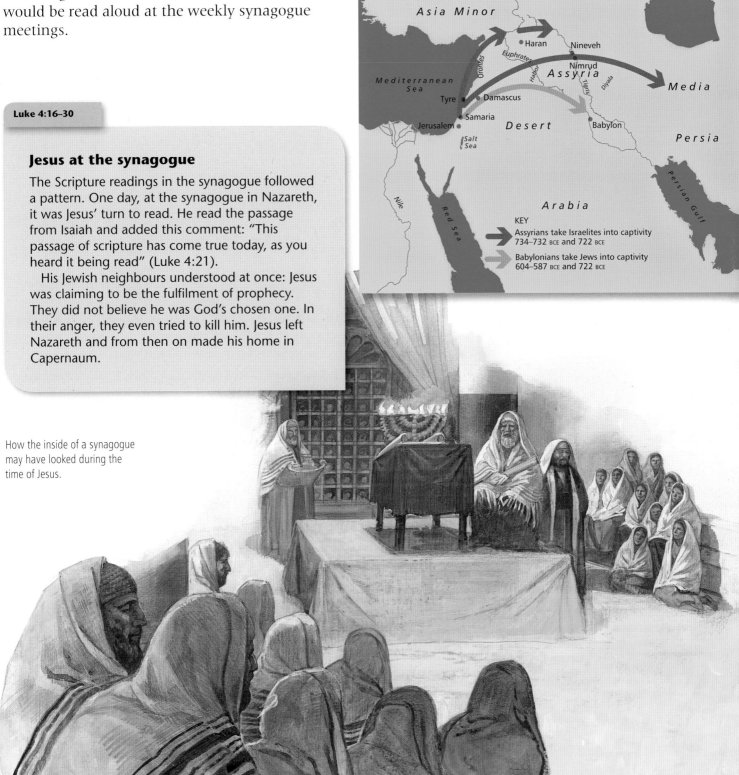

Luke 4:16–30

Jesus at the synagogue

The Scripture readings in the synagogue followed a pattern. One day, at the synagogue in Nazareth, it was Jesus' turn to read. He read the passage from Isaiah and added this comment: "This passage of scripture has come true today, as you heard it being read" (Luke 4:21).

His Jewish neighbours understood at once: Jesus was claiming to be the fulfilment of prophecy. They did not believe he was God's chosen one. In their anger, they even tried to kill him. Jesus left Nazareth and from then on made his home in Capernaum.

Asia Minor

Haran
Nineveh
Euphrates
Nimrud
Orontes
Habor
Assyria
Diyala
Media
Mediterranean Sea
Tyre
Damascus
Tigris
Jerusalem
Samaria
Desert
Babylon
Persia
Salt Sea
Nile
Red Sea
Persian Gulf
Arabia

KEY
→ Assyrians take Israelites into captivity 734–732 BCE and 722 BCE
→ Babylonians take Jews into captivity 604–587 BCE and 722 BCE

How the inside of a synagogue may have looked during the time of Jesus.

JEREMIAH 1

Jeremiah was a prophet in the kingdom of Judah for around forty years – through the reign of several kings (from 627 BCE to 586 BCE): Josiah, Joahaz, Jehoiakim, Jehoiachin and Zedekiah.

The image of the potter would have been a familiar one to the Israelites, for this was the most popular trade in Bible times.

Warning to Judah

Josiah made great efforts to encourage his people to be faithful to God. However, he was not entirely successful, and Jeremiah gives anguished warnings that the enemies who surround them could come and crush Judah just as they had crushed Israel.

Look, the enemy is coming like clouds.
Their war chariots are like a whirlwind,
and their horses are faster than eagles.
We are lost! We are doomed!

Jeremiah 4:13

"The Lord says," [Jeremiah told the nation,] "'My people are stupid;
* they don't know me.*
They are like foolish children;
* they have no understanding.*
They are experts at doing what is evil
* but failures at doing what is good.'"*

Jeremiah 4:22

The prophet of doom

Many describe Jeremiah as "the prophet of doom" because of his warnings of destruction. But God also gave Jeremiah strong messages of hope, forgiveness and restoration (see chapters 31–33).

He told the people to mend their ways; to remember the laws given to the people so long ago to guide them.

The people did not pay attention. One day, Jeremiah knew that God was telling him to go and watch a potter at work at his wheel, shaping pots from wet clay. If the pot did not come out right, the potter would simply squash the clay down and start again (Jeremiah 18:1–12).

Clay in God's hands

God explained that the nations were like clay in his hands. God had the power to build them up or squash them down. If a nation were going awry like a failed pot, God would squash them·flat and start again.

Another time, God told Jeremiah to buy a finished clay jar, to call a meeting of priests and elders, and to smash the jar to pieces. "God is warning you," he explained. "If our nation goes on disobeying God, then God will smash them" (Jeremiah 19:10–11).

Jeremiah made himself very unpopular with his warnings and he was mocked and jeered at. There was even a plot to take his life (11:18–23).

King Jehoiachin takes Judah captive

However, the destruction that Jeremiah had warned of came nearer. Babylon's King Nebuchadnezzar dealt the nation a real blow during the reign of King Jehoiachin. He chose several thousand people to be his prisoners, selecting those who would be the most useful: the ones who had skills to serve in government or in the practical crafts and trades, and some who could fight in his army. He even took King Jehoiachin to Babylon.

Hope for the exiles

Jeremiah wrote a letter to those who had been taken into exile, telling them to work hard to make a good and useful contribution to the places where they lived. "One day," he said, "you will be allowed to return home. You will build a new nation."

The Lord says… "I will restore you to your land. I will gather you from every country and from every place to which I have scattered you, and I will bring you back to the land from which I had sent you away into exile."

Jeremiah 29:14

A letter burns

King Nebuchadnezzar put Jehoiachin's uncle king in Jerusalem: Zedekiah. He was not a godly man, nor was he a clever politician. He refused to obey orders from the mighty Babylonian king, and so Nebuchadnezzar planned an attack.

Zedekiah sent a message to Jeremiah asking if God might work a miracle to save the city. "No," was Jeremiah's reply. "The only way anyone will survive the attack is to go and surrender."

Zedekiah still refused to heed Jeremiah's warnings to surrender. Jeremiah asked his scribe Baruch to write out his warnings on a scroll. The king asked for it to be brought to him. He had no plans to read it, let alone heed the words. He simply cut it up and threw it on the fire in his room in the palace (Jeremiah 36:20–26).

Jeremiah's reception

Jeremiah's plain speaking got him into trouble with several officials of the royal court. They threw him into a dry well. Jeremiah would have died of hunger and thirst there but for the fact that an Ethiopian servant came and rescued him (Jeremiah 38:1–13).

Zedekiah burns Jeremiah's letter.

JEREMIAH 2

In 586 BCE the army of the Babylonian King Nebuchadnezzar came and destroyed Jerusalem and the Temple. Its treasures were carried away, including the ark of the covenant that contained the stone tablets on which the great laws had been written in the time of Moses. It was the symbol of the agreement that if the nation obeyed God's laws, then God would protect them.

All is not lost. Out of the ruins of Jerusalem will come scenes of rebuilding and restoration: "I will restore my people to their land and have mercy on every family; Jerusalem will be rebuilt, and its palace restored" (Jeremiah 30:18).

A new promise

Jeremiah's preaching included a new promise from God:

The new covenant that I will make with the people of Israel will be this: I will put my law within them and write it on their hearts. I will be their God, and they will be my people. None of them will have to teach a neighbour to know the Lord, because all will know me, from the least to the greatest. I will forgive their sins and I will no longer remember their wrongs. I, the Lord, have spoken.

Jeremiah 31:33–34

LAMENTATIONS

So the warnings of the prophets came true: Jerusalem and its Temple were destroyed; the people were finally exiled. The event marked the final destruction of the kingdom of Judah. Some people think that the prophet Jeremiah, who predicted this disaster, may have written Lamentations.

The five chapters of Lamentations are each a poem about this tragic event. They describe the horrors and brutality of the attack and the misery of life in the city that is now in ruins.

A plea for help

The cause of all this, the writer declares, is that people failed to live in obedience to God. Now they call to him for help.

Let us examine our ways and turn back to the Lord.
Let us open our hearts to God in heaven and pray,
"We have sinned and rebelled, and you, O Lord, have not forgiven us."

Lamentations 3:40–42

My tears will pour out in a ceaseless stream Until the Lord looks down from heaven and sees us.

Lamentations 3:49–50

Even so, a message of confident trust shines through.

The Lord's unfailing love and mercy still continue,
Fresh as the morning, as sure as the sunrise.
The Lord is all I have, and so in him I put my hope.

Lamentations 3:22–24

A picture of a ruined Jerusalem, in which people and animals compete for scraps and leftovers.

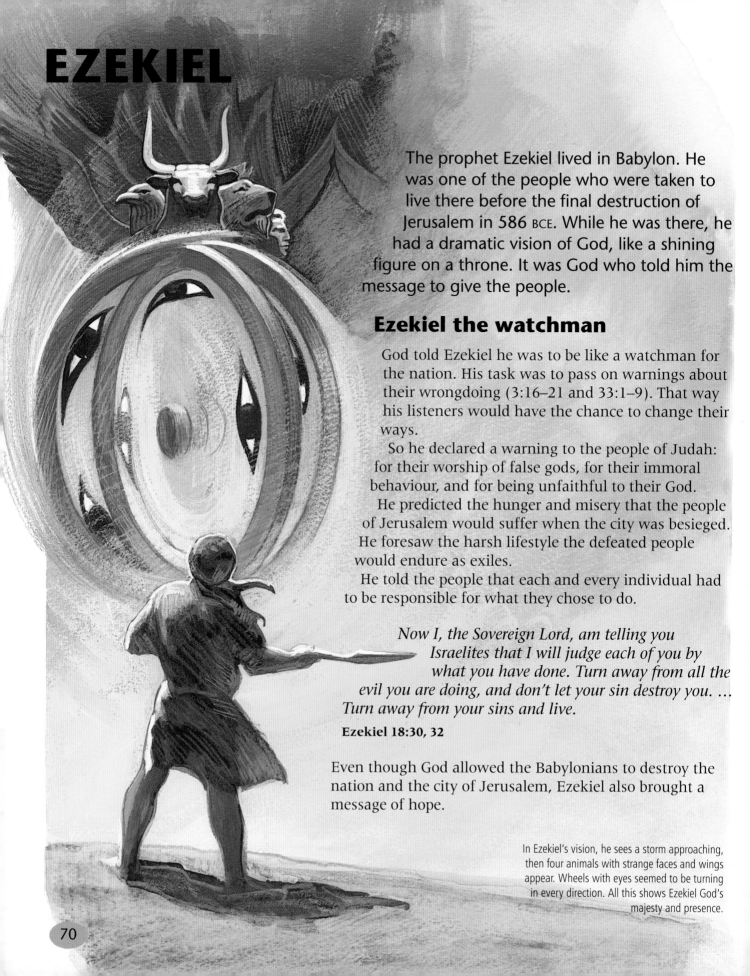

EZEKIEL

The prophet Ezekiel lived in Babylon. He was one of the people who were taken to live there before the final destruction of Jerusalem in 586 BCE. While he was there, he had a dramatic vision of God, like a shining figure on a throne. It was God who told him the message to give the people.

Ezekiel the watchman

God told Ezekiel he was to be like a watchman for the nation. His task was to pass on warnings about their wrongdoing (3:16–21 and 33:1–9). That way his listeners would have the chance to change their ways.

So he declared a warning to the people of Judah: for their worship of false gods, for their immoral behaviour, and for being unfaithful to their God.

He predicted the hunger and misery that the people of Jerusalem would suffer when the city was besieged. He foresaw the harsh lifestyle the defeated people would endure as exiles.

He told the people that each and every individual had to be responsible for what they chose to do.

Now I, the Sovereign Lord, am telling you Israelites that I will judge each of you by what you have done. Turn away from all the evil you are doing, and don't let your sin destroy you. … Turn away from your sins and live.

Ezekiel 18:30, 32

Even though God allowed the Babylonians to destroy the nation and the city of Jerusalem, Ezekiel also brought a message of hope.

In Ezekiel's vision, he sees a storm approaching, then four animals with strange faces and wings appear. Wheels with eyes seemed to be turning in every direction. All this shows Ezekiel God's majesty and presence.

70

Ezekiel the good shepherd

God described himself as the good shepherd of the scattered nation (just as Jesus is referred to as the good shepherd in John 10:7–18; see page 109):

I, the Sovereign Lord, tell you that I myself will look for my sheep and take care of them in the same way as shepherds take care of their sheep that were scattered and are brought together again.... I will lead them back to the mountains and the streams of Israel and I will feed them in pleasant pastures.... I myself will be the shepherd of my sheep, and I will find them a place to rest.... I will look for those that are lost, bring back those that wander off, bandage those that are hurt, and heal those that are sick...

Ezekiel 34:11–12, 13, 15–16

An imaginative image of Ezekiel in the valley of dry bones.

Dry bones

In another image, Ezekiel describes a valley of dried-up bones. The process of decay runs the other way: the bones become skeletons, then corpses, then living people. The prophet explains the meaning: that God will revive the nation that has been destroyed.

A king like my servant David will rule them forever.

Ezekiel 37:25

One day, Ezekiel declares, there will be a new Jerusalem (see Revelation 21) and a new Temple, and the name of the city will be "The Lord is here" (Ezekiel 48:35).

DANIEL

The book of Daniel is full of hope: it reminds its readers that God is more powerful than any ruler on earth, and that God will bring the final victory to his people.

The first six chapters contain stories of life in exile in Babylon.

God the rescuer

One story is that of three young Jewish men who were trained to work in King Nebuchadnezzar's court. Shadrach, Meshach, and Abednego did their jobs well, but they refused to bow down to the king's golden statue as he had ordered. For that disobedience they were thrown into a fiery furnace.

Then an amazing thing happened: the king saw the men walking round in the flames, in the presence of an angel. He ordered them to be pulled out of the fire, and they were unharmed.

Even Nebuchadnezzar was humbled. "There is no other god who can rescue like this," he declared (Daniel 3:29).

The king sees the three men walking around in the fiery furnace and is astonished. He is puzzled as to who the fourth person is: it is an angel of God who has come to protect them.

The writing on the wall

Other stories are about Daniel, who served Nebuchadnezzar and his son, Belshazzar.

One night, Belshazzar was enjoying a rowdy, drunken party. A hand appeared and began writing on the wall. Daniel was summoned to explain it.

"Mene mene" meant number. "Your days are numbered," said Daniel.

"Tekel" meant weight: "God has weighed you, and declared you a lightweight," he continued.

"Parsin" means divisions. "Your kingdom is going to be divided among your enemies, the Medes and Persians," he concluded.

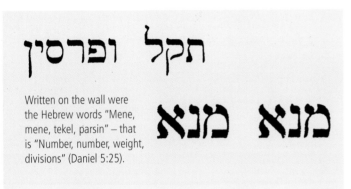

תקל ופרסין

מנא מנא

Written on the wall were the Hebrew words "Mene, mene, tekel, parsin" – that is "Number, number, weight, divisions" (Daniel 5:25).

In chapter 7, Daniel tells of a vision he has seen. In it there are four beasts (a winged lion, a bear, a leopard, and a mysterious and terrifying fourth one). Each animal symbolized a different threatening empire.

The words came true: that very night Cyrus took Babylon. Daniel went on to serve the next ruler, Darius the Mede. Enemies at court accused him of being more faithful to his God than to his king, and for this Daniel was thrown into a den of lions. But God sent an angel to protect Daniel, and the king ordered him to be brought to safety.

Darius, like Nebuchadnezzar before him, was forced to acknowledge God's greatness.

[Daniel's God] is a living God,
  and he will rule forever.
His kingdom will never be destroyed,
  and his power will never come to an end.
He saves and rescues;
  he performs wonders and miracles
  in heaven and on earth.

Daniel 6:26–27

The later chapters of Daniel describe the prophet's visions of things that are to come… of the kingdoms and empires that will rise and fall. Those of God's people who remain faithful will be kept safe:

When that time comes, all the people of your nation whose names are written in God's book will be saved. Many of those who have already died will live again: some will enjoy eternal life, and some will suffer eternal disgrace. The wise leaders will shine with all the brightness of the sky. And those who have taught many people to do what is right will shine like the stars forever.

Daniel 12:1–3

HOSEA

Hosea was another prophet who gave his message, mostly to Israel, during the reign of King Jeroboam II (2 Kings 14:23). What he said chimed with the miseries of his own life.

Israel's unfaithfulness

Hosea had a wife, Gomer, whom he loved dearly. She bore three children but also left him on several occasions for a string of lovers. Hosea was heartbroken, but he went on loving her. The time came when he took her back to his home, forgiven.

"This is what God has to say to you!" Hosea warned the people of Israel. "You are like Gomer was to Hosea. You have been unfaithful to God. Instead, you worship idols in the shape of bulls. You have no respect for what God wants."

He warned them that they would suffer for all this wrongdoing. Yet the manner in which he had forgiven Gomer was a sign: one day, the people would repent of their wrongdoing and God would forgive them.

Despite the heartache, God remains faithful to Israel, as Hosea was to Gomer. If the people turn away from their wrongdoing, they can be restored to God: "They will be alive with new growth… They will be fragrant like the cedars of Lebanon" (Hosea 14:6).

Minor prophets

HOSEA

JOEL

AMOS

OBADIAH

JONAH

MICAH

NAHUM

HABAKKUK

ZEPHANIAH

HAGGAI

ZECHARIAH

MALACHI

*The Lord says,
"I will bring my people back to me.
I will love them with all my heart;
no longer am I angry with them.
I will be to the people of Israel
like rain in a dry land.
They will blossom like flowers;
they will be firmly rooted
like the trees of Lebanon. …
The people of Israel will have nothing
more to do with idols;
I will answer their prayers and take care of them.
Like an evergreen tree I will shelter them;
I am the source of all their blessings."*

Hosea 14:4–5, 8

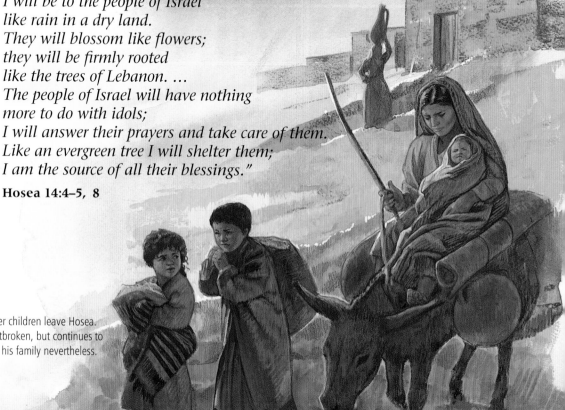

Gomer and her children leave Hosea. Hosea is heartbroken, but continues to faithfully love his family nevertheless.

JOEL

The book of Joel is hard to place. No one is quite sure when it was written or who the author was.

Many scholars think it dates to the time of the Persian empire (536–336 BCE), which is also the time when Nehemiah was involved in the rebuilding of Jerusalem.

Disaster swarms in

Joel describes a time of disasters in Judah. A swarm of locusts has invaded and eaten all the crops. The lack of rain means that no new harvest is growing. People and animals are desperate for something to eat.

The prophet describes the disaster as God's judgment on his people. If they admit to their wrongdoing they can be friends with God once more:

Come back to the Lord your God.
  He is kind and full of mercy;
  he is patient and keeps his
    promise;
  he is always ready to forgive and not punish.

Joel 2:13

God does not want to pour disasters on his people. Rather, he wants to pour out blessings. The day will come, says the prophet, when God will bless his people. At that time…

I will pour out my Spirit on everyone:
  your sons and daughters will proclaim my
    message;
  your old people will have dreams,
    and your young people will see visions.

Joel 2:28

Acts 2:16–21

The passage in Joel which sees God pouring out his Spirit (2:28) is the most famous part of the book. It was quoted by the apostle Peter when the followers of Jesus were filled with God's Spirit, on the day of Pentecost.

The invading swarms of locusts mentioned in Joel are a sign of God's judgment on the "Day of the Lord". The image of locusts being a symbol of doom is also used in Amos 7:1–3.

AMOS

One of the rulers of the northern kingdom of Israel was a man known as Jeroboam II (2 Kings 14:23). He reigned from 793 to 753 BCE. In that time he took control of the trade routes that passed through his kingdom. That gave him the power to make people pay to use them. Those of his people who were involved in all the comings and goings of trade had the chance to become wealthy. They began to buy up the land that belonged to poorer people. They built fine houses, planted vineyards, and enjoyed rich food and wine.

Amos was an outsider: a sheep farmer from the town of Tekoa, in the southern kingdom of Judah – a few kilometres away from Bethlehem. When he visited Israel, in around 760 BCE, he was shocked at what he saw.

The danger of riches

The rich were enjoying a life of luxury but they didn't care about justice for the poor.

They made a great show of being religious, and held elaborate services of worship, but they didn't pay attention to God's laws – which told them to treat everyone fairly.

"God's judgment is coming!" Amos warned them.

How terrible it will be for you that stretch out on your luxurious couches, feasting on veal and lamb! You like to compose songs, as David did, and play them on harps. You drink wine by the bowlful and use the finest perfumes, but you do not mourn over the ruin of Israel. So you will be the first to go into exile. Your feasts and banquets will come to an end.

Amos 6:4–7

Amos warns against gaining excessive riches at the expense of the poor.

OBADIAH

Invasion

A few decades later, this warning came true. King Shalmaneser of Assyria invaded the kingdom and sent its people to live in other parts of his empire. Other defeated peoples were brought to Israel to live (2 Kings 17).

Even so, the book of Amos does not end on a note of despair. "One day," Amos says, "God will rebuild the kingdom of David. The people will be able to rebuild their ruined cities" (Amos 9:11).

The book of the prophet Obadiah seems to belong to the period after the Babylonians destroyed Jerusalem, in 586 BCE.

It is addressed to the Edomites, whose kingdom lay south of Judah. Obadiah's prophecy accuses them of gloating over the attack on Jerusalem. They betrayed the people of Judah, capturing those who were trying to escape and handing them over to the invading army. When they saw that the city was utterly defeated the Edomites came and looted what they could.

The Edomites will be punished

One day, says God, the people of Judah will be strong again. They will reclaim their own land. They will occupy the territories around as well – including the land of Edom.

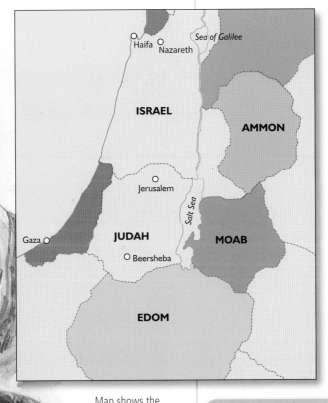

Map shows the location of Edom in relation to other nations.

The people of Jacob and of Joseph will be like fire; they will destroy the people of Esau as fire burns stubble.

Obadiah verse 18

Genesis 25:19–34, 27

The nation of Edom were descended from Esau, the twin brother of Jacob who had cheated him out of his inheritance. Jacob's descendants, the people of Israel and Judah, had for centuries been both neighbours and enemies.

JONAH (1–2)

The book of Jonah is among the shortest in the Bible. It is also distinctive in that it consists of just one story with a beginning, middle, and an end.

It is set in the period of history when the Assyrians ruled a great empire and threatened to conquer Israel. This fits with the reign of Jeroboam II of Israel – the society that Amos and Hosea criticized.

Jonah's disobedience

In the story, God tells a prophet named Jonah to go to Assyria's capital city of Nineveh. Jonah must warn the people that God has seen their wrongdoing and will punish them for it.

But Jonah sets off in the opposite direction. He doesn't want to give the people the opportunity to be forgiven by God. Instead he pays a sea captain the fare so he can sail to Spain. While the boat is at sea, God sends a storm. Jonah has to confess to the sailors that the storm is God's way of ending Jonah's journey, and they must throw him into the sea.

The storm abates even as Jonah is sinking down into the deep. God sends a great fish to swallow him whole. Alive and terrified, Jonah promises that if God saves him he will go to Nineveh.

Ruins at the ancient city of Nineveh. God told Jonah to tell his message to the Assyrians there. According to the Bible, the city was so large it took three days for Jonah to walk through it.

Above: Jonah is thrown overboard before being swallowed by a large fish.

Right: God planned for Jonah to go from Gath-hepher to Nineveh, only for Jonah to plan to head in the opposite direction to Tarshish.

Tarshish

Nineveh

Gath-hepher

④

①

Mediterranean Sea

② Joppa

③

JONAH (3–4)

Back to Nineveh

The fish vomits Jonah onto a beach, and the prophet sets off to deliver his message. The king and the people of Nineveh at once agree to mend their ways. God does not send any punishment.

Jonah's prayer

Jonah prays a furious prayer:

> *Lord, didn't I say before I left home that this is just what you would do? That's why I did my best to run away to Spain! I knew that you are a loving and merciful God, always patient, always kind, and always ready to change your mind and not punish. Now then, Lord, let me die. I am better off dead than alive.*

Jonah 4:2–3

He builds a little shelter and sits inside gloomily. The sun is hot, and he is very glad when God makes a plant grow quickly to shade it. A worm eats the stem, the plant wilts, and again Jonah is furious.

"If you can feel sorry about a plant," God tells him, "you can understand why I feel sorry about Nineveh: its people, its children, and all its animals" (Jonah 4:10–11).

A lesson for always

Although set in the time of the Assyrian empire the story of Jonah also had a message for a later time in the history of the Jewish nation. Around 400 BCE they had been released from exile and were resettling Jerusalem and the land they had called home. In the meantime, foreigners had made their home in the land, and the Jews had to work out how to live alongside them. The message of Jonah is that God cares for non-Jews – Gentiles – as well as Jews.

A hot and busy metalworks prepares to make more weapons, ready for the attack of the Assyrians (Micah 4:3–4).

MICAH

The prophet Micah lived at the same time as Isaiah – when Jotham, Ahaz, and Hezekiah were kings of Judah.

The enemy at the gates

It was the time when the Assyrians threatened and eventually destroyed the kingdom of Israel. Micah warned that Judah was going to suffer the same defeat. Already the enemy was at the gate of Jerusalem.

The reason was clear: in both Judah and Israel, people have been unfaithful to God. The powerful exploit the weak and leave the poor even poorer. They worship false gods.

The books of Isaiah and Kings tell of how God acted to save Jerusalem from the Assyrians, but Micah's message remained important when Jerusalem fell to the forces of Babylon years later.

Micah's message was one of warning – that Jerusalem would be destroyed (3:12) – but also one of hope for the future, and echoes that of Isaiah (27:10):

And so, because of you, Zion will be ploughed like a field, Jerusalem will become a pile of ruins, and the Temple hill will become a forest.

Micah 3:12

The Temple

One day, the Temple in Jerusalem would be a place of pilgrimage for anyone who wanted to live by God's standards. Respect for God would lead to world peace.

[The Lord] will settle disputes among the nations,
* among the great powers near and far.*
They will hammer their swords into ploughs
* and their spears into pruning knives.*
Nations will never again go to war,
* never prepare for battle again.*
Everyone will live in peace
* among their own vineyards and fig trees,*
* and no one will make them afraid.*

Micah 4:3–4 (see also Joel 3:10)

A ruler for Israel

All this will happen when God's chosen king is born and at last the people will live in safety:

The Lord says, "Bethlehem Ephrathah, you are one of the smallest towns in Judah, but out of you I will bring a ruler for Israel, whose family line goes back to ancient times."

Micah 5:2

A man in traditional dress views Bethlehem in the distance.

Matthew 2:1–6

The Gospel of Matthew quotes the line that God's king will be born in Bethlehem. The Gospel writer is keen to show that Jesus is indeed the long-promised king.

81

NAHUM

The book of the prophet Nahum rails against the kingdom of Assyria and speaks about God's coming judgment on wickedness.

It appears to be set in the seventh century BCE, when Assyria had destroyed the kingdom of Israel and still threatened the kingdom of Judah.

Nineveh threatened

The message is devastating and clear: God is about to destroy Assyria's capital, Nineveh. Judah will not fall to its armies.

The Lord is good;
he protects his people in times of trouble;
he takes care of those who turn to him.
Like a great rushing flood he completely destroys his enemies;
he sends to their death those who oppose him.

Nahum 1:7–8

In the past, Assyria's army had been greatly feared. Now another army was going to destroy it in the same way it had destroyed others. Nahum describes the awfulness of the war.

Listen! The crack of the whip,
the rattle of wheels,
the gallop of horses,
the jolting of chariots!
Cavalry troops charge,
swords flash, spears gleam!
Corpses are piled high,
dead bodies without number…

Nahum 3:2–3

The mighty, fearsome, and godless Assyrian empire was extremely prosperous. Its vast wealth is evidenced in the entrances to many of the Assyrian palaces being decorated with large winged creatures, such as below, which is being transported from the quarry by huge numbers of men.

Nineveh

An important city in the Assyrian empire with 120,000 inhabitants. In 722 BCE the Assyrians had devastated Israel and now the prophets foretold that God would allow Nineveh to be destroyed by the Babylonians.

HABAKKUK

This book belongs to the time when the Babylonians were beginning to wage war to make themselves a superpower. In fact, they were to replace the Assyrians as the great rulers of the world.

Words of Josiah picked up by Habakkuk

The people of Judah must have been surprised. Around the time that Zephaniah gave his warnings, a king named Josiah had discovered just how much he and his people had forgotten God's laws. He had ordered sweeping changes to make the people obey the laws and keep the festivals (2 Kings 22, 23; see pages 42–43).

Habakkuk warns that Josiah's best efforts have not worked as he hoped. Still people fight and quarrel. The laws are not enforced and no one can get justice.

As a result, warns the prophet, God will allow the Babylonians to destroy the people.

Living as God wants

This was his key message:

Those who are evil will not survive, but those who are righteous will live because they are faithful to God.

Habakkuk 2:4 (see also Hebrews 10:35–39; Romans 1:16–17; Galatians 3:11)

But despite these warnings, Habakkuk does end on a happier note:

*Even though the fig trees have no fruit
and no grapes grow on the vines…
I will still be joyful and glad,
because the Lord God is my saviour.*

Habakkuk 3:17–18

Viewed as a symbol of peace and prosperity (1 Kings 4:25), the failure of the fig tree to flourish would have been seen as a disaster.

ZEPHANIAH

The opening line of this book identifies Zephaniah clearly: he is the great grandson of King Hezekiah. He speaks his message in the godless time before King Josiah's reforms.

King Hezekiah had had to put his trust in God. When the Assyrian army was camped outside Jerusalem, he could only hope for a miracle. A miracle happened: sickness swept through the Assyrian army and they set off for home without attacking the city. In this way the kingdom of Judah survived (see pages 40–41).

The day is coming

Trust in God, it seems, did not last. People still worshipped other gods. Zephaniah criticizes the wealthy people of Jerusalem as being concerned only about having fine houses and plenty of wine. He warns them that the day is coming when God will punish them, and the equally godless nations around them.

The awful destruction will not be the end. Zephaniah tells of God's promise for the future of Jerusalem, where Solomon's Temple stood on a hilltop terrace.

I will remove everyone who is proud and arrogant, and you will never again rebel against me on my sacred hill. I will leave there a humble and lowly people, who will come to me for help. The people of Israel who survive will do no wrong to anyone, tell no lies, nor try to deceive. They will be prosperous and secure, afraid of no one.

Zephaniah 3:11–13

The awesome power of the Assyrian army is shown in this relief. The army is attacking a fortified city with a battering ram and soldiers are also tunnelling through the wall.

HAGGAI

This short book dates to not long after the first group of Jews had returned from exile to Jerusalem, around 538 BCE.

Time to rebuild

The pioneers had a great deal to do. Although they began to rebuild their lives with enthusiasm and laid the foundations for a new Temple, they soon stopped work on them. Instead they put their efforts toward what seemed to be more practical matters: building houses for themselves and trying to grow crops.

However, the weather has been unfavourable, and the harvests have been very poor.

"Don't you understand why?" explains the prophet. "It is because the people have neglected to rebuild the Temple."

This failure is a sign that they are not putting God first. When they do, everything will change. God gives this message of hope:

See what is going to happen from now on. Although there is no grain left, and the grapevines, fig trees, pomegranates, and olive trees have not yet produced, yet from now on I will bless you.

Haggai 2:18–19

The Temple was finally completed by around 520 BCE: "The new Temple will be more splendid than the old one, and there I will give my people prosperity and peace" (Haggai 2:9).

As the Jews returned to Jerusalem, they experienced prosperity under God's blessing, and set about rebuilding their homes.

ZECHARIAH

The book of Zechariah belongs, like Haggai, to the time when the exiles returned to Jerusalem.

The early chapters are a series of visions, reminding readers of why the people of Jerusalem have suffered at the hands of their enemies.

Long ago I gave these commands to my people: "You must see that justice is done, and must show kindness and mercy to one another. Do not oppress widows, orphans, foreigners who live among you, or anyone else in need. And do not plan ways of harming one another." But my people stubbornly refused to listen.

Zechariah 7:9–11

Shout for joy!

But that is in the past. God's plan for the future is to send a new king.

Shout for joy, you people of Jerusalem!
Look, your king is coming to you!
He comes triumphant and victorious,
but humble and riding on a donkey…

Zechariah 9:9

Good shepherd

The one whom God sends is also described by Zechariah as a good shepherd (11:7). He is killed, and the flock scattered. Yet after that the time will come when God returns with his angels as king over all the earth (Zechariah 14:9).

The Prince of peace

Christians have seen in the book of Zechariah a prediction of the life and work of Jesus. One example of this is the image of the "Prince of peace" riding into Jerusalem on a donkey (Matthew 21:4–5) and "the one they have pierced" (Zechariah 12:10, NIV), which is quoted in John 19:37. Zechariah 9:9 is also quoted in John 12:15.

MALACHI

The book of Malachi is about life in the rebuilt Jerusalem, probably just after the time of Nehemiah.

In chapter 1, God emphasizes his love for Israel, ("I have always loved you", verse 2). But then comes a stern rebuke to priests and people.

Even the priests are being disrespectful in the way they conduct worship at the Temple and in the example they set.

Down the wrong path

"… you priests have turned away from the right path," [warns the prophet]. *"Your teaching has led many to do wrong."*

Malachi 2:8

Malachi

The title of this book is taken from 3:1, which refers to "my messenger". Malachi means "my messenger".

Destruction of the wicked

The people, too, have failed to live by God's standards. The prophet reminds them that they should be building strong families in which children can learn to live as God's children.

One day, warns the prophet, God's judgment will strike. The wicked will be destroyed.

But for you who obey me, my saving power will rise on you like the sun and bring healing like the sun's rays.

Malachi 4:2 (compare Luke 1:78)

An impression of how the rebuilding work in Jerusalem might have been carried out, with stone being taken from quarries for the rebuilding of the Temple.

THE SCRIPTURES COME INTO BEING

No one can say for sure when any of the contents of the Old Testament were first written down.

Written in stone

The earliest reference to anything being written down comes with the great Commandments, carved into stone for Moses to carry to the people. However, these laws were something the priests were expected to treasure. They in turn could teach the people to know the Law and to obey it.

Culture in the royal court

It was only when David united the people in a well-defended kingdom that there was much time for cultural activities. David is credited with writing some of the Psalms, and his son Solomon is linked to the authorship of Proverbs, Ecclesiastes, and the Song of Songs.

Histories of the kings

It is likely that the first history books were written in the time of King Solomon. When the kingdom divided, both the northern kingdom of Israel and the southern kingdom of Judah kept a written record of the kings (see pages 34–35 on 1 Kings 12–22).

Storytelling

From ancient times to this day, storytelling has been part of human culture. Stories can be about real events or they can be made up for a particular purpose: to make a point, to teach someone a lesson, and so on. It is likely that many of the Bible stories first existed as stories that were told aloud and passed on from one generation to the next. This handing down of stories told aloud is called the "oral tradition".

How the historians may have worked during the time of King Solomon.

The words of the prophets

The prophets whose words are included in the Scriptures gave their message at different times and in different places. Some would have had followers who carefully recorded what they said. Jeremiah even had a scribe named Baruch (Jeremiah 36:32).

King Josiah finds a scroll

When King Josiah ruled in Judah, a neglected scroll was found in the Temple. The king had it read aloud and was shocked to discover how he and the people had neglected the Law simply because they did not know it. Clearly, someone, at some point, had begun collecting the writings of the nation (2 Kings 22).

In exile

When the people of Judah were taken off to live in exile in Babylon (597 to 537 BCE), they were separated from the Temple and the chance to worship God there. They had to show their faithfulness to God in other ways. They began to treasure the stories of their past and to meet together to learn from them.

Ezra

Ezra was a priest and scholar who played a leading role in the resettlement of the land. He made sure that the Scriptures were read out to the people. Books of the Bible that had been written in Hebrew were translated into the language they now spoke: Aramaic.

The Dead Sea Scrolls

In 1947 a shepherd boy discovered fragments of scrolls in the dry, rocky cliffs by the Dead Sea in Israel (as shown in this picture). His find led to the discovery of many ancient scrolls dating from before the time of Jesus. Copies of the Scriptures, including the so-called Isaiah Scroll (see pages 4–5), were among them.

THE SCRIPTURES IN GREEK

From the time of the exile to Babylon (from 597 BCE), Jews made their home in different regions of the victorious empire (see map on page 65). They did not all return to Judah when the Persian emperor allowed them to do so. When Alexander the Great defeated the Persians and set up his own Greek empire, there were communities of Jews in many places.

Synagogues

The exiles who were taken to Babylon had met on the riverbank to worship God and celebrate their Jewish faith. As Jewish communities grew in size and influence in the Greek empire, they built meeting places: the synagogues. Each wanted to have copies of the Scriptures, so that the people could learn their faith. A special cupboard to store them in became the key feature of every synagogue.

Above: A silver coin bearing the head of Alexander the Great.

Right: This stone was discovered in the main hall of a synagogue dating from the first century CE – one of the oldest synagogues discovered yet. It was located on the shore of the Sea of Galilee. It is carved on five sides, one side depicting a seven-branched menorah (see page 28).

The Pharisees

A strict religious sect, the Pharisees were devoted to keeping God's laws. Many were against Jesus and saw him as a threat (see Matthew 22:15–33 and 23:1–39).

The traditional clothing of a Pharisee.

Reading the Scriptures

In the synagogues men took it in turns to read the Scriptures to the congregation. In line with tradition, the Gospels refer to Jesus taking his turn (see also box on page 65).

Luke 4:16–20

A Greek translation

Greek was the language spoken by all peoples throughout the Greek empire. Jews at this time had to relearn Hebrew, the language of their Scriptures, even to be able to read them.

The answer, of course, was to have the Hebrew words translated into Greek. In the middle of the third century BCE the Jews who lived in the Egyptian town of Alexandria put the idea to their king, Ptolemy II Philadelphus. He wanted to have the support of the Jews and agreed to fund their plan.

Seventy scholars

Seventy scholars who knew both Hebrew and Greek worked on the translation of the Scriptures. It became known as the Septuagint, from the Latin word for seventy.

Codex Sinaiticus (above) is a fourth-century manuscript of the Greek Bible, written between 330 and 350 CE. Originally it contained the whole of both testaments, but today only portions of the Greek Old Testament (or Septuagint) survive, along with a complete New Testament.

Ptolemy authorizing the Greek translation of the Hebrew Scriptures.

THE DEUTEROCANON

A Bible consists of a collection of books that at some stage have received the official approval of elders of the faith. This is sometimes called the "canon" of Scripture. The word indicates that they measure up to the right standard to be included.

The prefix "deutero-" simply means "second". The deuterocanon therefore means the "second list". The reason for there being a second list goes back to the Greek translation (see pages 90–91).

(see pages 90–91)

Apocrypha

The word "Apocrypha", meaning "hidden things", is also used to refer to the books of the Deuterocanon.

What is a scroll?

In the time of the Greek empire, seventy scholars set about making a translation of the Hebrew Scriptures into Greek. They were given boxes of scrolls to work on, and they translated everything contained in the boxes.

Their translation, the Septuagint, became the Old Testament of the Bible approved in the early centuries of the Christian faith.

Some time after, it was discovered that their collection had more books in it than the Hebrew Bible. The translators had translated more books simply because they had found them.

Protestant and Catholic

In the sixteenth century, in Europe, there was just one branch of Christianity – the Roman Catholic Church. Some Christians began taking a fresh look at the Bible. They protested that the Roman Catholic Church had lost track of the faith and what it meant. These Protestants set up their own branches of the faith, and decided only to include in their Bible the books that were in the Hebrew Bible.

The Catholics chose to keep all the books that were in the Septuagint.

For many years the arguments between Protestant and Catholic were bitter. In recent times both Protestants and Catholics have preferred to focus on what they agree on.

The Deuterocanon is generally regarded as useful to read and it is respected even though some think it does not measure up as well as the main canon.

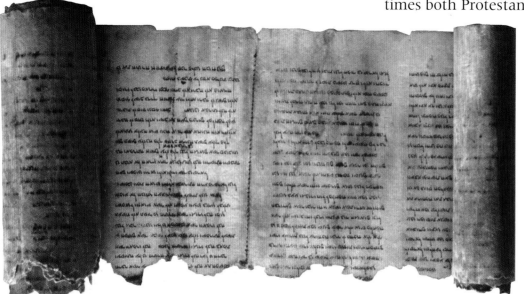

The books of the Deuterocanon

Books of the Septuagint that are included in the canons of the Eastern Orthodox and Roman Catholic Churches	Books in the Septuagint that are not included in the Roman Catholic canon, but are accepted by the Eastern Orthodox Church	A book in the Slavonic (old Russian) Bible and in the Latin Vulgate appendix
Tobit	1 Edras	2 Edras
Judith	Prayer of Manasseh	
Additions to the Book of Esther	Psalm 151	
Wisdom of Solomon	3 Maccabees	
Ecclesiasticus, or the Wisdom of Jesus son of (ben) Sira(ch)	4 Maccabees	
Baruch		
The Letter of Jeremiah		
Additions to the Book of Daniel: The Prayer of Azariah and the Song of the Three Jews Susanna Bel and the Dragon		
1 Maccabees		
2 Maccabees		

Apocrypha

In the Protestant Bible, the Deuterocanonical books can be found in between the Old and New Testament; in the Roman Catholic Bible they are found threaded through the Old Testament.

A close-up of a page from the Septuagint, containing the text of Daniel 11:40–45.

Examples of Deuterocanonical text

Pride has its beginning when a person abandons the Lord, his maker.

Ecclesiasticus 10:12

Look at the rainbow and praise its Creator!
How magnificent, how radiant, its beauty!
Like a bow bent by the hands of the Most High,
it spans the horizon in a circle of glory.

Eccelesiasticus 43:11–12

1 & 2 MACCABEES

The books of the Deuterocanon known as Maccabees describe important events in history that fall in the 400 years between those described in the Old Testament and the New.

But you, my sons, be strong and courageous in defending the Law, because it is through the Law that you will earn great glory.

1 Maccabees 2:64

The Temple is robbed

The first book of Maccabees states that the Persian emperor Darius was defeated by the invading Alexander the Great. Alexander put some of his generals in charge of the defeated nations. The descendant of one of these generals was Antiochus IV Epiphanes. He in turn (in 167 BCE) marched against Jerusalem and stripped all the treasure from the Temple. As a Gentile, he had no respect for the Jewish faith.

One man, Mattathias, was overcome with grief at what had happened. Before he died, he asked his sons to remember the great heroes of their nation and to be as bold.

Antiochus IV Epiphanes

A Seleucid king, he encouraged Greek ideas and culture; his attempts to suppress Judaism caused the War of the Maccabees (167–164 BCE).

Judas Maccabeus

Judas was the son who took his father's place in the family. He lived at a time when the Greeks had conquered the land of the Jews. He raised an army to defeat the forces of the Gentiles. Then he went to Jerusalem to put everything in the Temple to rights. When it was done, they held a festival to celebrate. This festival of dedication lasted eight days.

In 2 Maccabees 10, Judas Maccabeus and his followers recapture the Temple and Jerusalem. They are horrified to find the Temple's altar dedicated to foreign gods and set about purifying the Temple and rededicating it to God.

Jesus and the festival of the rededication of the Temple

The festival established by Judas Maccabeus continued through the years, and continues to this day as the Jewish festival of Hanukkah. As a Jew himself, Jesus was at the Temple in Jerusalem for one particular festival, and the event is noted in John's Gospel: "It was winter, and the Festival of the Dedication of the Temple was being celebrated in Jerusalem. Jesus was walking in Solomon's Porch in the Temple".

John 10:22–23

The Hasmonean dynasty that ruled Judea included descendants of the Maccabee family. Here are some examples of Hasmonean pottery, discovered in the Hasmonean palace in Jericho.

Bust of Apollo, the Greek god of the sun. The Greeks oppressed the Jews and placed statues of their gods in Jewish places of worship.

Left: Judas Maccabeus engaged in several battles against the Gentiles, one of which was against a Timothy and his army at Maspha, as depicted here.

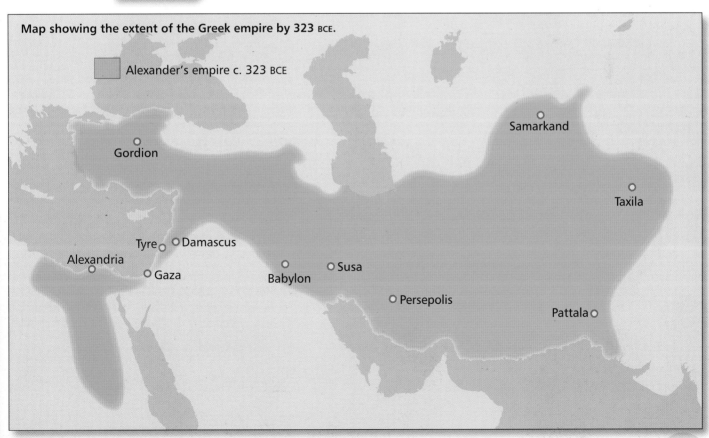

Map showing the extent of the Greek empire by 323 BCE.

Alexander's empire c. 323 BCE

Samarkand

Gordion

Taxila

Tyre Damascus

Alexandria

Gaza Babylon Susa

Persepolis

Pattala

THE NEW TESTAMENT

The New Testament contains books about Jesus and his followers. Although Jesus spoke Aramaic, it is mainly written in Greek.

The word "testament" means covenant. Jesus himself talks about the new covenant that he establishes by the spilling of his blood at the crucifixion. It puts the seal on the new promise God makes to people, to let Jesus' death be their forgiveness and to welcome them into a new kingdom (see 1 Corinthians 11:23–25 and Luke 22:14–23, Matthew 26:26–30, and Mark 14:22–26).

The book of Acts tells how the message about Jesus spread throughout the world. Luke, travelling with the apostle Paul, saw many people accept the message. Their writings make up a considerable bulk of the New Testament.

The accounts of the life of Jesus

Among the books are four accounts of the life of Jesus: the Gospels of Matthew, Mark, Luke, and John.

There is also another book written by Luke. This book, the Acts of the Apostles, tells of the first followers of Jesus and their mission to spread the news about him (see Acts, pages 112–13).

After that are twenty-one letters from some of the first Christians (see pages 116–43) and a piece of writing that describes a vision of the end of time: the book of Revelation (see pages 144–45).

The synoptic Gospels

Three of the Gospels are referred to as "synoptic" Gospels, as they all tell the story from a similar point of view. The shortest Gospel, of Mark, was almost certainly the first to be written and it focuses on Jesus' work during the years he was a preacher in Galilee. It seems that the writers of Luke and Matthew used it to create their own Gospels.

Matthew and Luke also share some material that does not appear in Mark. Scholars describe this as coming from some other source that we no longer have. It is referred to as "quelle" or simply "Q".

Each of the three Gospels also has some material not found elsewhere. The chart on the next page explains this further.

Gospel

The word "Gospel" means "good news". The Gospels give details about the birth, life, ministry, and death of Jesus.

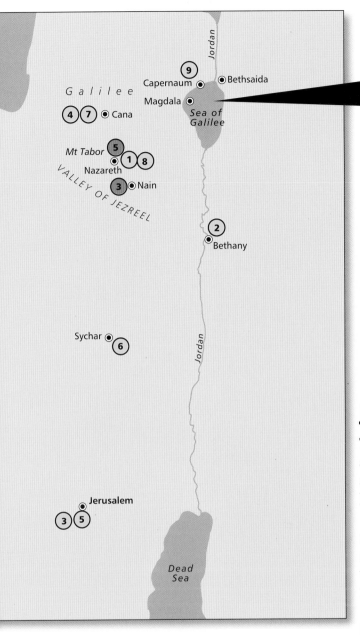

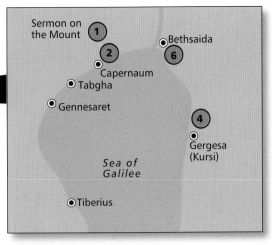

Above: **Places where key events took place in the second year of Jesus' ministry.**

1) Jesus preaches the Sermon on the Mount
2) Performs several miracles at Capernaum
3) Raises to life the dead son of a widow at Nain (see map, left)
4) Delivers two demon-possessed men from unclean spirits
5) Returns to Nazareth (see map, left)
6) Feeds a large crowd of 5,000 and leaves Galilee for Tyre and Sidon

John

The Gospel of John takes quite a different approach. Much of the action takes place in and around Jerusalem. Much more space is given to long speeches, or discourses, that Jesus makes.

Strikingly, the description of the final meal Jesus shares with his disciples before the crucifixion does not mention Jesus sharing the bread and wine to explain the new covenant (compare Luke 22:19–20, for example).

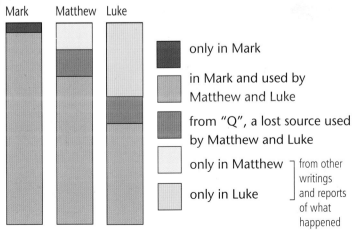

Above: **Places where key events took place in the first year of Jesus' ministry.**

1) Jesus leaves his childhood home
2) Baptized by John the Baptist in the River Jordan
3) Tested by the devil in the desert, and tempted to throw himself off the highest point of the Temple at Jerusalem
4) Changes water into wine at a wedding
5) Visits Jerusalem and cleanses the Temple
6) Talks with a Samaritan woman
7) Meets a royal official at Cana and heals his son, who was sick, at Capernaum
8) Thrown out of the synagogue in Nazareth
9) Moves to Capernaum, calls his disciples, and teaches in the vicinity of Capernaum, performing many miracles

Above: This chart shows what material is particular to each of the three Gospels.

MATTHEW 1

A man named Papias, writing around 130 CE, said that Matthew wrote his book in Hebrew or Aramaic. These were the languages best known to the Jews of Jesus' day, which matches the fact that Matthew was writing for people who knew and respected the old Jewish Scriptures: Jewish Christians.

Prophecies come true

One of the distinctive features of Matthew's Gospel is the way the author sets out to make it quite clear to his readers that in Jesus the promises God made through the prophets are coming true. All through his Gospel he refers back to the Old Testament Scriptures to underline this same point. One example of this is:

Do not think that I have come to do away with the Law of Moses and the teachings of the prophets. I have not come to do away with them, but to make their teachings come true.

Matthew 5:17

The wise men

One of the unique things about Matthew's Gospel is the story of the wise men who follow a star (chapter 2).

They come to Jerusalem seeking the newborn king of the Jews. The ruling king, Herod, feels threatened. He knows very well that the Jewish people believe the words of their prophets and are expecting a king like David – God's messiah. He asks his advisors this question: "Where will the Messiah be born?" "In the town of Bethlehem in Judea," they reply. "For this is what the prophet wrote." They go on to quote a passage from the book of Micah (5:2):

*Bethlehem in the land of Judah,
you are by no means the least of the leading cities of Judah;
for from you will come a leader
who will guide my people Israel.*

Matthew 2:6

It is there that Herod sends the wise men, and it is there that they find Jesus.

A view of modern-day Bethlehem.

A model of Herod's Temple in Jerusalem. It was made of marble and was built on the highest hill in the city — the Temple Mount.

The Mount of Beatitudes, Tabgha. Overlooking the Sea of Galilee, it is thought to be the site where Jesus gave the Sermon on the Mount.

The Sermon on the Mount

Messiah/Christ

These two words mean the same thing: "an anointed one" – God's chosen king. "Messiah" is the word that comes from the Hebrew language; "Christ" comes from the Greek.

Chapters 5 to 7 of Matthew's Gospel are often referred to as the Sermon on the Mount. They are a presentation of Jesus' key teachings on how his followers should live. Those who obey are part of his true kingdom: the kingdom of heaven (for more on the kingdom of heaven, see Matthew 2, pages 100–101). There is a strong link between these teachings and the older teachings of the Jewish scriptures.

Read Luke 6:17–46

Luke's Gospel contains a similar set of teachings to the Sermon on the Mount but they are described as being preached in a level place and are sometimes called the Sermon on the Plain.

Jesus tells his listeners what leads to true happiness in 5:3–11:

> *Happy are those whose greatest desire is to do what God requires;*
> *God will satisfy them fully!*

Matthew 5:6

He tells them that they must go further than the Law requires in doing good:

> *You have heard that it was said, "Love your friends, hate your enemies." But now I tell you: love your enemies and pray for those who persecute you, so that you may become the children of your Father in heaven.*

Matthew 5:43–55

Right: Huge crowds gather to listen to Jesus' so-called Sermon on the Mount.

MATTHEW 2

Jesus tells his listeners how to pray –
sincerely and without making a show
of being religious, and gives them one
prayer in particular:

Our Father in heaven:
 May your holy name be honoured;
  may your Kingdom come;
  *may your will be done on earth as it is in
   heaven.*
Give us today the food we need.
Forgive us the wrongs we have done,
  *as we forgive the wrongs that others have
   done to us.*
Do not bring us to hard testing,
  but keep us safe from the Evil One.

Matthew 6:9–13

He also warns of the dangers of riches:

*Do not store up riches for yourselves here on
earth, where moths and rust destroy, and robbers
break in and steal. Instead, store up riches for
yourselves in heaven, where moths and rust
cannot destroy, and robbers cannot break in and
steal.*

Matthew 6:19–20

The kingdom of heaven

The writer of Matthew records the many ways in
which Jesus described the kingdom of heaven.
Here is one example:

*The kingdom of heaven is like this. A man takes
a mustard seed and sows it in his field. It is the
smallest of all seeds, but when it grows up, it
is the biggest of all plants. It becomes a tree,
so that birds come and make their nests in its
branches.*

Matthew 13:31–32

The kingdom of heaven is also likened to a fine
pearl (13:45–46), treasure hidden in a field
(13:44), and a king who prepared
a wedding banquet for his son
(22:2).

Matthew 9:18–19, 23–26 tells the story of the miracle of Jairus' daughter who had died. Jairus shows great faith in being convinced that should Jesus place his hand on her, she would come back to life. This is exactly what happened. The story is also found in Mark 5:21–24, 35–43 and Luke 8:40–42, 49–56.

The kingdom is not described as a territory like other kingdoms. It is rather the overall effect of people obeying Jesus' teaching and living as God's people.

Following Jesus

The writer of Matthew also reminds its readers of what it means to be a follower of Jesus. That person needs to be humble, willing to serve others, and to forgive wrongdoing. They must be totally dedicated to God and willing to give away their possessions to be so (Matthew 5:23–26).

The kingdom of heaven

A central theme in Matthew's Gospel, "the kingdom of heaven" is referred to thirty-two times.

The end times

The Gospel of Matthew also presents what Jesus said about the end of time. There will be a final judgment:

Then the King will say… "Come and possess the kingdom which has been prepared for you ever since the creation of the world. I was hungry and you fed me, thirsty and you gave me a drink; I was a stranger and you received me in your homes, naked and you clothed me; I was sick and you took care of me, in prison and you visited me."

Matthew 25:34–36

Left: In Matthew 22, Jesus compares the kingdom of heaven to a wedding banquet. He explains that those who are invited to the feast, but who repeatedly refuse to attend, will eventually be cast out and others invited instead.

MARK

Mark is the shortest of the Gospels, and probably the first to be written down – perhaps in 65–70 CE.

An ancient tradition says that it was written by a follower of Jesus named John Mark, and that he based his book on things that Simon Peter himself had told the first followers of Jesus.

Following the action

Mark's account of the life of Jesus focuses on the action – the things Jesus actually did – beginning with his years in Galilee.

Among the memorable things Mark records are many miracles: Jesus heals people who are unwell (2:1–12), brings a little girl back to life (5:22–24, 35–43), calms a storm with just a command (4:35–41), and walks on water (6:45–52).

Miracles

Jesus performed many miracles in his lifetime. They were considered to be "mighty works" and he used them to show people that he was the Son of God.

Above: One of the most well-known miracles in Mark's Gospel is that of Jesus' healing of blind Bartimaeus (10:46–52). As Jesus passes him, Bartimaeus calls out, "Jesus! Son of David!", affirming his faith that Jesus was the Messiah. In healing him, Jesus confirmed, "Go, your faith has made you well."

The green and lush area of the Jordan springs at Caesarea Philippi, where the River Jordan begins, was well known for having lots of idols of pagan gods. It is here that Jesus asked his disciples whom they thought he was.

Son of God, Messiah

Miraculous events are among those chosen to help convince readers of Mark's clear belief about Jesus, which he states right at the start: "This is the Good News about Jesus Christ, the Son of God."

It includes the episode when Jesus asks his disciples who people think he is, and Peter gives his very direct answer: "You are the Messiah" (Mark 8:29) – see picture bottom left.

Jesus in Jerusalem

The later chapters of the book are about Jesus' final visit to Jerusalem: Jesus' crucifixion and his resurrection. Mark doesn't want his readers to think of these events as a defeat. Instead, he carefully notes that Jesus predicted his own death and said it was part of God's plan, having been foretold in the Scriptures.

John Mark

The author of the Gospel is thought by many to be the John Mark who features in the stories of Jesus' followers. The book of Acts describes him as the young cousin of a believer named Barnabas. They were both companions to the apostle Paul on the first journey Paul took to spread the news about Jesus.

John Mark left the trip early, and went home to Jerusalem. For that reason Paul didn't want to take him on the next trip. Barnabas disagreed with this decision, and Paul and Barnabas fell out in a big argument.

After that, Barnabas took John Mark as his companion and Paul took a man named Silas.

All those involved remained loyal to Jesus, and it seems likely they mended their friendship.

Acts: 13 (especially verses 4 and 13); 14; 15 (especially verse 37)

When Jesus is dying, people come and mock him.

Let us see the Messiah, the king of Israel, come down from the cross now, and we will believe in him!

Mark 15:32

By contrast, the Roman soldier who watches Jesus die sees things differently.

"This man was really the son of God!" he said.

Mark 15:39

Mark's Gospel ends rather abruptly: the Sunday after Jesus' death, some women go to his tomb. It is empty, but an angel tells them that Jesus is alive and going to Galilee.

Two endings

There are two later endings that have been added on to the Gospel. Both of them complete the story with Jesus himself appearing to his disciples and telling them to spread his message to the world.

The "Garden Tomb", traditionally said to be the site of Jesus' tomb, which was empty when Mary Magdalene, Mary the mother of James, and Salome went to visit Jesus' body (Mark 16:1–8).

LUKE 1

The Gospel of Luke is the longest of the accounts of Jesus' life in the New Testament.

The author is generally thought to be the Gentile Christian named Luke who travelled with Paul on his journeys. This same Luke wrote the book of Acts (see pages 112–13). Paul mentions Luke in several letters (2 Timothy 4:11; Philemon 24). In one he describes him as "our dear doctor" (Colossians 4:14).

Luke writes at the opening of his account that his book is for "Theophilus". The name is Greek and the whole book is clearly written so that Gentiles can understand it, even though they wouldn't know a great deal about the Jewish faith.

He says that he has researched his book carefully and spoken to people who were actually there in the time of Jesus. It is even possible he spoke with Jesus' mother, Mary.

Jesus' birth

Luke and Matthew are the only two Gospels to describe the birth of Jesus, and Luke's account contains details that are at the heart of Christmas plays: the angel Gabriel's visit to Mary to announce that she is to be the mother of God's own son; the journey to Bethlehem with Joseph; and the couple having to shelter in a stable.

Mary cradles her baby in a manger, and it is there that shepherds come and find him when angels tell them the good news of his birth.

Luke 3:21–22; Matthew 3:13–17; Mark 1:9–11

John the Baptist

John the Baptist was an important man in the life of Jesus. The son of Zechariah and Elizabeth, he was Jesus' cousin, and baptized him in the River Jordan before Jesus began his ministry.

On the advice of an angel of God, the shepherds visit the newborn Jesus in the stable.

See pages 100–101

The Lord's Prayer

The Lord's Prayer in Luke's Gospel has slightly different wording to that of Matthew, as seen here.

Jesus said to them, "When you pray, say this:

'Father:
    May your holy name be honoured;
    may your Kingdom come.
Give us day by day the food we need.
Forgive us our sins,
    for we forgive everyone who does
    us wrong.
And do not bring us to hard
    testing.' "

Luke 11:2–4

Matthew's Lord's Prayer

This, then, is how you should pray:

"Our Father in heaven:
    May your holy name be honoured;
    may your Kingdom come;
    may your will be done on earth as
    it is in heaven.
Give us today the food we need.
Forgive us the wrongs we have done,
    as we forgive the wrongs that
    others have done to us.
Do not bring us to hard testing,
    but keep us safe from the Evil
    One."

Matthew 6:9–13

Jesus' boyhood

Luke is the only Gospel to speak of Jesus as a boy. It tells of the time when he was twelve and went to Jerusalem with Mary, Joseph, and other pilgrims from Nazareth for the Passover festival.

When the festivities are over the group set off for home. They travel a whole day before Mary realizes that Jesus isn't with them. Mary and Joseph return to Jerusalem and find him in the Temple, talking with some of the most important teachers about the Jewish faith. Jesus is surprised that Mary is so worried about him: "Didn't you know that I had to be in my Father's house?" he says (Luke 2:49).

Jesus and the poor

Luke's Gospel emphasizes Jesus' concern for the poor and the disadvantaged. Jesus says:

The Spirit of the Lord is upon me, because he has chosen me to bring good news to the poor. He has sent me to proclaim liberty to the captives and recovery of sight to the blind, to set free the oppressed...

Luke 4:18

Luke 6:20–21 and Luke 7:22

The Holy Spirit

Luke often speaks about the Holy Spirit. For example, it is because of the power of the Holy Spirit that Mary becomes pregnant (1:35), and the Holy Spirit comes down from heaven to Jesus when he is baptized (3:22). It is also by the power of the Holy Spirit that Jesus is able to begin his work as a preacher (4:14).

Luke's second book, the book of Acts, describes how God's Holy Spirit helps and strengthens those who wish to be followers of Jesus.

From a young age, Jesus followed his earthly father, Joseph, in his trade of carpentry.

105

LUKE 2

Some of the best-loved parables that Jesus told are found only in Luke (see chart opposite).

The Prodigal Son

The parable often known as "The Prodigal Son" is one of these (Luke 15:11–32). In it, the son who squanders his share of the family money is welcomed home by his forgiving Father. It is typical of Luke to want to tell his readers of Jesus' concern for people who had gone astray, and whom God wants to welcome into his kingdom.

The parable of the Good Samaritan (below) is another. In this story, Jesus shows people what it means to love your neighbour, as the Law requires. It is not about being religious; it means noticing people in need and doing practical things to help. That the person who shows genuine love is a Samaritan and not a Jew would have been important to Luke's Gentile readers (see Luke 10:25–37).

The Samaritans

In Jesus' time, the Samaritans, who lived in Samaria (in between Galilee in the north and Judea in the south), were not liked by the Jews – in fact they were sworn enemies. They were descended from those who had settled in Israel after it had been conquered by Assyria in 722 BCE (see pages 40–41). It was significant that Jesus should use the example of the Samaritan in his story: Jesus' followers should love everyone, whatever their background.

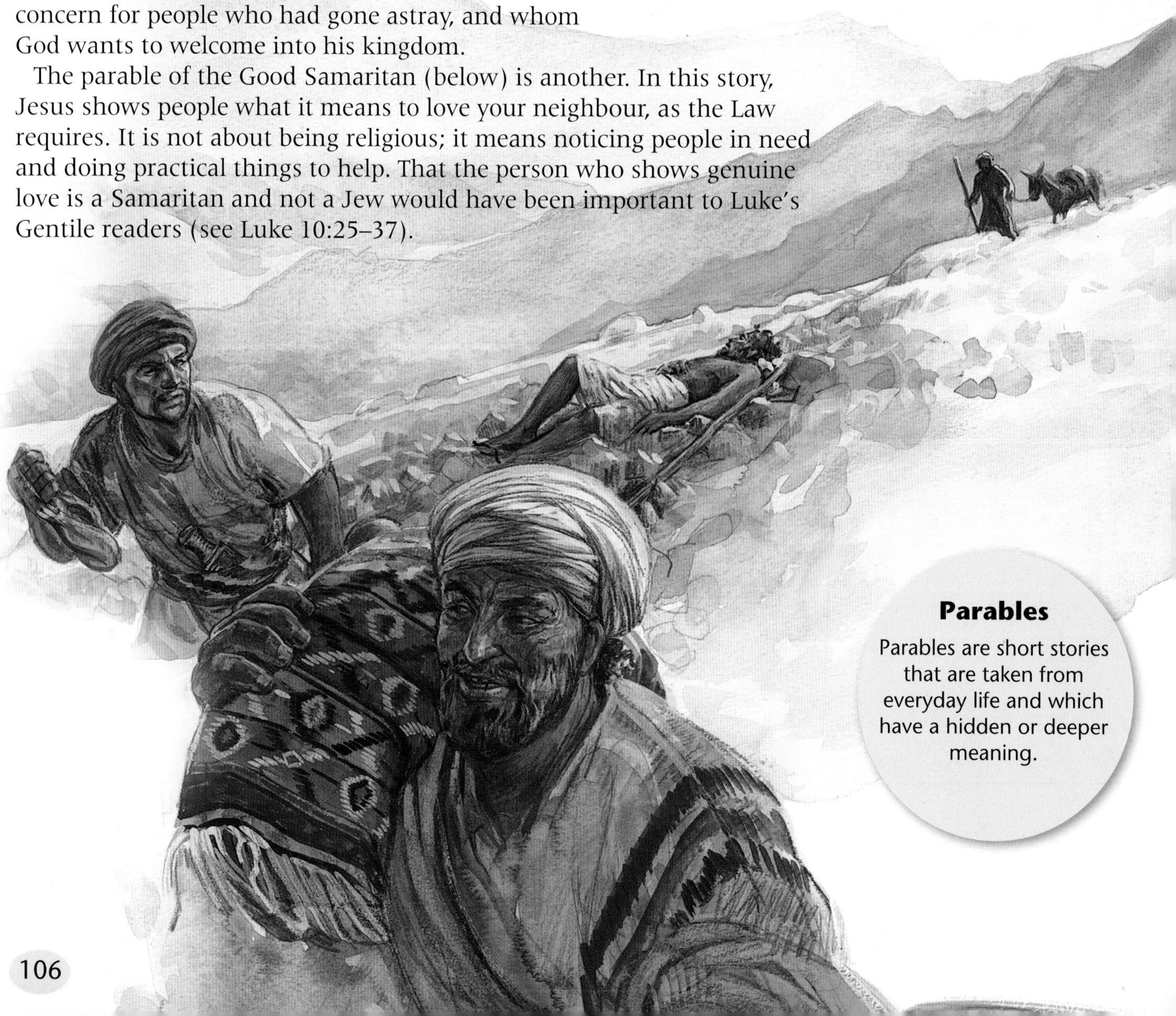

Parables

Parables are short stories that are taken from everyday life and which have a hidden or deeper meaning.

Here are all the parables that Jesus told:

Parable	Matthew	Mark	Luke
Lamp under a bushel	5:14–15	4:21–22	8:16; 11:33
Houses on rock and on sand	7:24–27		6:47–49
New cloth on an old garment	9:16	2:21	5:36
New wine in old wineskins	9:17	2:22	5:37–38
Sower and soils	13:3–8	4:3–8	8:5–8
Tares	13:24–30		
Mustard seed	13:31–32	4:30–32	13:18–19
Leaven (yeast)	13:33		13:20–21
Hidden treasure	13:44		
Pearl of great value	13:45–46		
Drag-net	13:47–48		
Lost sheep	18:12–13		15:4–6
Two debtors (unforgiving servant)	18:23–34		
Workers in the vineyard	20:1–16		
Two sons	21:28–31		
Wicked tenants	21:33–41	12:1–9	20:9–16
Marriage feast; man without a wedding garment	22:2–14		
Fig tree as herald of summer	24:32–33	13:28–29	21:29–32
Ten "bridesmaids"	25:1–13		
Ten talents (Matthew) or Pounds (Luke)	25:14–30		19:12–27
Sheep and goats	25:31–46		
Seedtime to harvest		4:26–29	
Creditor and the debtors			7:41–43
Good Samaritan			10:30–37
Friend in need			11:5–8
Rich fool			12:16–21
Alert servants			12:35–40
Faithful steward			12:42–48
Fig tree without figs			13:6–9
Places of honour at the wedding feast			14:7–14
Great banquet and the reluctant guests			14:16–24
Counting the cost			14:28–33
The lost coin			15:8–10
The prodigal son			15:11–32
Dishonest steward			16:1–8
Rich man and Lazarus			16:19–31
The master and his servant			17:7–10
The persistent widow and the unrighteous judge			18:2–5
The Pharisee and the tax collector			18:10–14

JOHN 1

The Gospel of John is probably the last of the Gospels to have been completed, perhaps around 90 CE.

According to ancient tradition, it was written by John, the disciple of Jesus. The author had a very clear aim in selecting what to include, stating this:

In his disciples' presence Jesus performed many other miracles which are not written down in this book. But these have been written in order that you may believe that Jesus is the Messiah, the Son of God, and that through your faith in him you may have life.

John 20:30–31

The result is a Gospel unlike the others: everything is told to make a clear point about who Jesus is.

In addition, nearly half the Gospel consists of Jesus teaching and explaining what his message is, and what people need to do to gain "eternal life".

I am

The Gospel of John includes seven claims that Jesus made about himself, each beginning "I am…", and each helping to build up a picture of who Jesus was.

I am the bread of life (6:35)

Jesus has fed a huge crowd with just five loaves and two fish. He then sails away across Lake Galilee, but the people come and find him, hoping for more free food. Jesus tells them that he did not come to save them from being physically hungry, but from a spiritual hunger for meaning and purpose.

"I am the bread of life," he explains. "Those who come to me will never be hungry; those who believe in me will never be thirsty."

"I Am"

In the Old Testament God is called "I Am" (Exodus 3:14). God says to Moses, "I am who I am. You must tell them: 'The one who is called I Am has sent me to you.'" Jesus is therefore making quite a claim in using the same wording.

I am the light of the world (8:12)

Jesus' miracles (or "signs" as they are called in John's Gospel) and teaching make him popular with many people. However, the religious leaders mistrust him and think he is not respectful of the old teaching they know so well. Jesus declares this to them:

I am the light of the world… Whoever follows me will have the light of life and will never walk in darkness.

An impression of the miracle of feeding a huge crowd of 5,000 with just five loaves and two fish.

Water into wine

John's Gospel contains the only account of Jesus at a wedding, in a place called Cana. Jesus' mother, Mary, is there, and she tells Jesus that the wine is about to run out. She wants him to help.

Jesus asks the servants to fill six large jars with water. Then he tells them to take out a cupful for the man in charge to taste. Jesus has turned the water into wine and the man says it is of the finest quality.

John 2:1–10

Terracotta wine jars like those mentioned in the story at Cana.

I am the gate for the sheep (10:7) and I am the good shepherd (10:11)

The old Scriptures of the Jewish people had already described God as the shepherd of people (see Psalm 23, Ezekiel 34:11–31, and Zechariah 11). John's Gospel records Jesus using the same picture language: he is the gate for the sheep – the way in and out of the fold. Those who try to break into the sheepfold any other way are thieves and robbers.

He is the good shepherd. He is the one whom his flock follow, and he is ready to die to keep them safe.

I am the resurrection and the life (11:25–26)

On one occasion, Jesus visits two friends, Mary and Martha, whose brother, Lazarus, has died. Martha is in grief because Jesus did not come sooner to heal him.

Jesus makes this declaration: "I am the resurrection and the life. Those who believe in me will live, even though they die."

He then goes on to work a miracle in bringing Lazarus back to life.

I am the way, the truth, and the life (14:6)

At the final meal he shares with his disciples, Jesus says that he is going to his Father's house to prepare a place for them. The one named Thomas is puzzled: he doesn't know where Jesus is going. Jesus replies, "I am the way, the truth, and the life; no one goes to the Father except by me."

I am the real vine (15:1)

Later, on the evening of the Last Supper, Jesus uses another picture, this time from wine-making. Jesus is the root of the vine, and his followers must remain attached to him if they are to live good and fruitful lives.

The funeral of Lazarus. When he heard the news of his friend's illness, Jesus delayed visiting until after Lazarus has died, to the puzzlement of Mary and Martha and the disciples. This, said Jesus, was so that the disciples would believe – he is indeed the resurrection and the life.

JOHN 2

Light and love

Two of the themes that run right through John's Gospel are those of light and love. In 3:16, the writer says, "For God loved the world so much that he gave his only Son, so that everyone who believes in him may not die but have eternal life." Right at the very beginning of the Gospel, in the section that is known as the "Prologue", Jesus is portrayed as a light who shines in the darkness – he offers light to all: "The Word [that is, Jesus] was the source of life, and this life brought light to people" (1:4).

The Last Supper

John describes a final meal Jesus shares with his disciples before the crucifixion. His account is distinctive in that it begins with Jesus doing the work of a servant and washing his disciples' feet. He tells them that they should be willing to follow his example and serve one another in humble ways (John 13:1–16). Jesus says, "Now that you know this truth, how happy you will be if you put it into practice!" (John 13:17).

Above: In this fifteenth-centry fresco, Jesus washes the disciples' dusty feet before the Last Supper. This is an act that was traditionally done by slaves (see 1 Samuel 25:41). Jesus therefore makes himself the disciples' slave.

Above: An inscription in stone reading "Pontius Pilate, Prefect [governor] of Judea". It was Pilate who reluctantly condemned Jesus to death (right) – but not before washing his hands: a symbol that he was not responsible for this judgment.

The new commandment

At the Last Supper Jesus shares with his disciples, he warns them that he will soon be put to death. He gives them a new commandment: "… love one another. As I have loved you, so you must love one another. If you have love for one another, then everyone will know that you are my disciples."

Hours later, Judas betrayed Jesus. The other disciples fled. Peter followed as closely as he dared to the house of the high priest. When challenged, he denied knowing Jesus.

**John 13:34–35;
18:15–27**

Having realized that the stranger on the shore who had helped the disciples catch fish was the risen Jesus, Peter runs to greet him. "Do you love me?" asked Jesus, three times. "Yes, you know I love you," replied Peter each time. At this, Jesus said to Peter that he should look after his followers (21:15–17).

Jesus and Peter

The Gospel of John ends with a story of the time after Jesus had died and had been resurrected. Peter and six other disciples did not know what to do, so they went to Galilee, and went fishing as they used to do.

Jesus met them on the shore. He asked Peter to be the new shepherd of his flock of followers (John 21).

ACTS

The book of Acts carries on where the Gospel of Luke (see pages 104–106) leaves off. As with the Gospel, the author is almost certainly the same Luke who travelled with Paul. There are even places in the book where the author uses the word "we", showing that he was part of Paul's group (for example, Acts 20:6).

Like the Gospel, the book begins with a letter to "Dear Theophilus". It sums up the message of the earlier book. Just as Luke wanted to make it clear that the things that Jesus did were by the power of the Holy Spirit, so the work of Jesus' disciples will depend on the same Holy Spirit. In Acts 1:8, Jesus says, "When the Holy Spirit comes upon you, you will be filled with power, and you will be witnesses for me in Jerusalem, in all of Judea and Samaria, and to the ends of the earth."

Pentecost

Chapter 2 describes the time when the disciples really took on the task Jesus had set them. From the time he was crucified they had been afraid that those same religious leaders who had arranged for Jesus' arrest and execution would hunt them down too, so they tried to stay out of sight. One day, when they were in a room together, they heard a rushing wind and saw tongues of fire above their heads. They knew they were filled with the Holy Spirit, and had the courage and confidence to go out and spread the news about Jesus.

Peter delivers a passionate sermon during the meeting at Pentecost, affirming that Jesus is the Messiah.

Above: The believers who witnessed the Holy Spirit had come from all over the world. Suddenly, the disciples were able to speak in the languages of all the other believers present.

When Jesus chose twelve people to be his close followers he called them his disciples: people who would learn from their teacher. After Jesus left this world his close followers were known as "apostles": people who had been sent as messengers.

Peter

The early chapters of Acts (1–12) have mostly to do with Peter and the other disciples spreading the good news in Jerusalem. They are despised by the official teachers of the Jewish faith, who treat them cruelly.

Eventually they are forced to leave Jerusalem. In a vision, Peter, who was later to become the leader of the church, realizes that God wants the message to be spread to Gentiles as well as Jews (Acts 10:9–16).

Having received the Holy Spirit at Pentecost, Peter heals a lame man.

Saul

A chief enemy of the church in Jerusalem is a man named Saul (Acts 8:1–3). He is on his way from Jerusalem to Damascus to hunt down believers when he is blinded by a light and hears the voice of Jesus speaking to him (Acts 9). This dramatic event leads him to change his mind: to be converted. He is baptized and starts preaching.

He goes on to become a missionary for the faith: an apostle.

He travels with a variety of companions on three main journeys around the empire (Acts 13; 16; 19). His work, combined with that of other apostles, leads to the setting up of groups of Christians in many different places: churches.

Below. As the message of Jesus spread rapidly, more and more people became Christians. The Jewish religious leaders felt threatened. A young Christian named Stephen was charged and found guilty of blasphemy; he was sentenced to death by stoning. Among the witnesses was a man called Saul, later Paul the apostle. This incident may have paved the way for Saul's later dramatic conversion to Christianity.

PAUL'S TRAVELS

Rome

Puteoli

ITALIA

Rhegium

SICILIA

Syracuse

MALTA

MACEDONIA

Amphipolis
Thessalonica
Philippi
Neapolis
Berea
Apollonia

ACHAIA

Troas
Assos

MYSIA

Mitylene
Pergamum
Thyatira
Sardis

Corinth
Cenchreae
Athens

PHRYGIA

GALATIA

Ephesus

ASIA

Antioch

LYCAONIA

Miletus

Colossae

PISIDIA

Iconium

Cnidus

LYCIA

Perga
Lystra
Derbe

To Rome

Rhodes

Attalia

CILICIA

Phoenix

CRETE

Myra

Tarsus

Fair Havens

Salmone

CYPRUS

Antioch

Lasea

Salamis

Seleucia

SYRIA

Paphos

Sidon

1st Journey (46–47 CE)

2nd Journey (50–52 CE)

Tyre

3rd Journey (53–57 CE)

Ptolemais

Journey to Rome (57 CE)

Caesarea

Alexandria

Jerusalem

0   500 km

0   300 miles

EGYPT

Map showing the three major
missionary journeys that Paul and
his companions undertook across the
empire.

At first, Paul spent some time in Galatia, and then preaching in Damascus and Jerusalem. He felt called by God to travel around the empire, spreading the good news about Jesus. Along the way, he founded and led many Christian churches and wrote many letters to stay in touch with the believers.

On his first missionary journey, Paul visited Cyprus, Antioch, and Galatia with his companion Barnabas. He began to preach the message to the Gentiles, and with Silas, on his secound journey, he toured Asia Minor and Greece, which included Athens, Corinth, and Ephesus.

During his third journey, he travelled around Asia Minor, and visited Ephesus where he stayed for three years before returning to Rome.

Paul and Barnabas embark on Paul's first missionary journey, sailing from Seleucia in Syria.

Paul's companions on his missionary journeys included:

Barnabas	Apollos
John Mark	Titus
Timothy	Peter
Silvanus (Silas)	James

LETTERS FROM CHRISTIANS

The New Testament of the Bible includes twenty-one letters. They were written by leading Christians to help new believers understand more about their faith.

By now the apostles were travelling far and wide to spread the news about Jesus. In many places they set up a church: a group of believers who would meet together to encourage one another.

One way for the apostles to stay in touch and give advice about matters of the day was to write to them. Letters were written on papyrus or parchment that could be folded up, tied, and sealed.

Letters across the empire

There was no regular mail service. Each letter was taken to its destination by a messenger.

Of course, the government of the Roman empire in Rome needed to stay in touch with the regions. It had its own private delivery service for official documents. The network of roads and shipping routes helped the apostles and their messengers.

Many of the letters were written by the apostle Paul to particular churches or people. These letters often talk about particular questions or problems.

Others were written as open letters, for any and every church. These talk more generally about what it means to follow Jesus.

Both sorts were highly valued by those who received them. All of these letters were probably copied out by the recipients so that they could be shared with other churches nearby.

Right: Writing materials from the time of the Roman empire, including a shale tablet, an inkwell and styli.
Opposite: Paul asks his friend Tychicus to deliver a letter to Ephesus. The letter was sent round all the churches in the area.

Paul's letters

- ROMANS
- 1 AND 2 CORINTHIANS
- GALATIANS
- EPHESIANS
- PHILIPPIANS
- COLOSSIANS
- 1 AND 2 THESSALONIANS
- 1 AND 2 TIMOTHY
- TITUS
- PHILEMON

General letters

- HEBREWS
- JAMES
- 1 AND 2 PETER
- 1,2, AND 3 JOHN
- JUDE

A view of Ephesus, in modern-day Turkey; a former Greek city. The road is Marble Street, which leads to the Great Theatre where Paul may have preached during his stay in Ephesus. On the left is the Commercial Agora. Roman roads such as this would have enabled faster travel around the empire, which meant that missionaries such as Paul, Silas, and Peter, could travel around more easily spreading the message of Jesus.

ROMANS

The letter named Romans is one of the letters of Paul. It is addressed to Christians in the capital city of the empire: Rome itself.

The church was not one Paul had set up. No one is quite sure how the news about Jesus reached Rome. It may have been from people who heard the message in Jerusalem on the day of Pentecost.

How to be God's children

The church in Rome included both Jews and Gentiles. Paul wrote to explain that both could live as friends of God. The good news he had to share was this:

Many Roman homes and public buildings had floors decorated with intricate mosaic designs showing aspects of everyday life. Here, the mosaic depicts one of the favourite pastimes of the era: gladiator fighting.

… the gospel reveals how God puts people right with himself: it is through faith from beginning to end. As the scripture says, "The person who is put right with God through faith shall live."

Romans 1:17

He is referring to a passage from the book of Habakkuk:

Those who are evil will not survive, but those who are righteous will live because they are faithful to God.

Habakkuk 2:4

The Romans gave the world many important engineering inventions, including aqueducts, such as this one found in Caesarea. They established aqueducts in over 200 cities around the empire, and their installation allowed clean water to be brought into a city and dirty water to be taken away.

He goes on to explain that no one is righteous because they always fall short of God's standards, despite always striving to keep God's laws. God simply forgives those who believe in Jesus (Romans 4).

God helps those who believe by sending his Holy Spirit to live in them. "Those who are led by God's Spirit are God's children," he explains (Romans 8:14).

How to live as God's children

Faith, Paul explains, is what matters. However, those who have faith and God's Spirit should live as the Spirit guides them. They must love one another, be forgiving of those who do them wrong, and be willing to do humble tasks:

Love must be completely sincere. Hate what is evil, hold on to what is good.

Romans 12:9

Try to do what everyone considers to be good. Do everything possible on your part to live in peace with everybody.

Romans 12:17–18

Shipwrecked

Although Paul did not set up the church in Rome, he was eager to go to the most important city in the empire (Romans 15:22–33).

He did get there in the end, but only because of his legal battle with the authorities in Jerusalem. He argued that he was a Roman citizen and had the right to be put on trial in the emperor's court.

The book of Acts describes his journey there, as a prisoner. On the voyage, the ship was wrecked off the coast of Malta. He and other passengers had to swim to shore to save themselves (Acts 27:27 – 28:1).

When at last he came near the city, the Christians there were eager to meet him.

On the journey to Rome, Paul and his friends' ship encountered severe storms before running aground. Paul assured them that God would protect them all. All on board managed to swim ashore to an island they discover is Malta.

1 CORINTHIANS

During his second missionary journey the apostle Paul himself established the church in Corinth (Acts 16). Situated on the Greek peninsula, it had been an important place during the time of the Greek empire. Now it was part of the Roman empire. Most of its inhabitants were Gentiles who were from diverse backgrounds.

In the years since Paul had moved on, the church had grown but its members had begun to quarrel: about what to believe; about what it meant to live as a follower of Christ; about how to worship as a Christian.

One body, many parts

Paul wrote his letter to deal with all these issues. He described the church as a body with many parts. Each part depends on the other. Like parts of the body, members of the church may have different tasks and different abilities, but they are all equally important (see 1 Corinthians 12:12–31).

The Lord's Supper

Paul reminds his readers of the importance of the ceremony of the "Lord's Supper", recalling the instructions Jesus gave his disciples at the Last Supper.

During the Roman period Corinth, with its two harbours, was an important city that had good communication links to the Mediterranean area. Here, the Acrocorinth, an acropolis (citadel), overlooks the ancient city.

For I received from the Lord the teaching that I passed on to you: that the Lord Jesus, on the night he was betrayed, took a piece of bread, gave thanks to God, broke it, and said, "This is my body, which is for you. Do this in memory of me." In the same way, after the supper he took the cup and said, "This cup is God's new covenant, sealed with my blood. Whenever you drink it, do so in memory of me."

1 Corinthians 11:23–25

Eucharist

"Eucharist" is another name for the "Lord's Supper". It comes from the Greek word meaning "to give thanks". It symbolizes the new covenant given by God.

Matthew 26:17–30; Mark 14:12–26; Luke 22:7–23; John 13:1–30

2 CORINTHIANS

The letter in the Bible known as 2 Corinthians is not actually the second letter Paul wrote to the Christians of Corinth. In 2 Corinthians he talks about another letter he had sent to put their Christian faith on the right track and that he had clearly upset many. Now he wants to mend the relationship and to encourage the Corinthian Christians in their faith.

He speaks of his plan to visit the church again, and his hope that all the troubles in the church will have been settled by then.

Early Christians meet together to share a meal as they did in Acts 2:46. The bread and wine in a meal took on special significance because of Jesus' instructions to remember him.

GALATIANS

Below left: The harbour of Attalia (Antalya) in modern Turkey is still a busy marina today. This was one of the places that Paul visited with Barnabas on his first missionary journey.

Paul's first missionary journey took him to the Roman province of Galatia (see Acts 13 and 14). He and his companion Barnabas worked together to set up churches in several towns. Many of the believers were Gentiles.

Jewish customs

After Paul and Barnabas had left, Jewish believers had tried to "improve" on the teaching they had received. These Jews thought it important for the Gentiles to follow Jewish customs. In fact, Paul says in his letter, even Jesus' disciple Peter once held that view; Paul openly disagreed with him and told him clearly that it was wrong to force Gentiles to live like Jews (Galatians 2:14).

The Jewish law

At the heart of Jewish beliefs was obedience to the law. All the law can do, Paul argues, is show people that they can't keep to it. Jesus has changed all that. There is a new way to God.

And so the Law was in charge of us until Christ came, in order that we might then be put right with God through faith.

Galatians 3:24

Family and friends enjoy a shared meal together, embracing Paul's words in Galatians 5:14.

Freedom to live a holy life

Those who believe in Christ, says Paul, are free from the law. However, that freedom is not an excuse for bad behaviour of any kind.

Instead, let love make you serve one another. For the whole Law is summed up in one commandment: "Love your neighbour as you love yourself."

Galatians 5:13–14

In the mountainous region of Pisidian Antioch, Galatia, are the foundations of the synagogue where Paul gave his first recorded sermon. Later, the Church of St Paul was built on the remains.

Above: A Roman family enjoying their shared mealtime.

EPHESIANS

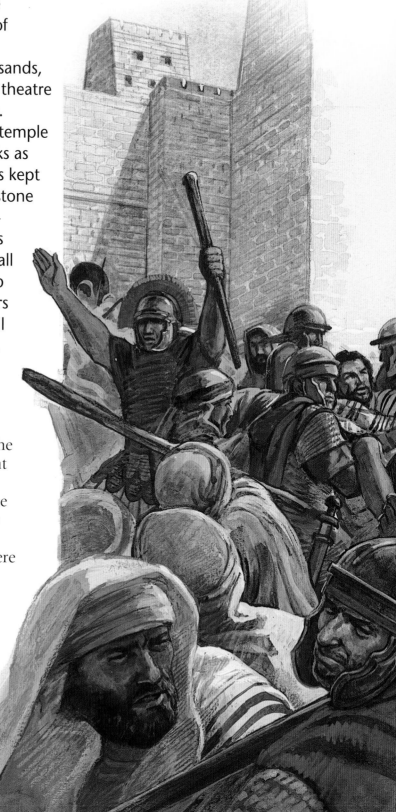

Ephesus was one of the largest cities in the Roman empire, situated where a number of routes that were useful for trade crossed.

It had a population of hundreds of thousands, and among its attractions was an open-air theatre cut into the hillside that could seat 24,000.

Most impressive of all, however, was its temple to the goddess Diana (known by the Greeks as Artemis). A statue of Diana was kept there, and it was cut from a "stone that fell down from heaven" – perhaps a meteorite (see Acts 19:35). Pilgrims came from all over the empire to worship there. Among the souvenirs they liked to buy were small silver statues of the goddess.

Paul in Ephesus

Paul's preaching of the news of Christianity in the town was seen as a threat to the cult of Diana. The book of Acts describes the anger of the silversmiths towards Paul. It led to a riot in which two of Paul's companions, Gaius and Aristarchus, were captured by the mob and marched off to the theatre. They might even have been killed if the town clerk hadn't acted to calm the whole thing down.

Even so, the church in Ephesus continued to meet and to grow. Most of the members were Gentiles.

Statues of the goddess Artemis were very popular in first-century Ephesus, and the famous Artemis temple there was considered to be one of the ancient wonders of the world.

The letter

Paul wrote his letter to the Ephesians after that eventful visit. At the time he was being held as a prisoner in Rome, waiting for his trial. He writes to remind them of the message at the heart of their faith: because of Jesus, they have been made friends of God.

He goes on to describe the kinds of lives they must lead: being controlled by love. He talks about how husbands and wives should love and respect one another, as should parents and children (Ephesians 5:21–33).

The armour of God

One striking feature of this letter is Paul's description of how Christians should "put on the armour of God" so they can resist attacks from all the forces of evil.

So stand ready, with truth as a belt… with righteousness as your breastplate, and as your shoes the readiness to announce the Good News of peace… carry faith as a shield… accept salvation as a helmet, and the word of God as the sword which the Spirit gives you.

Ephesians 6:14–17

Ruins along the Ephesian Curetes Street, leading to the Library of Celsus.

Left: Crowds rioting in Ephesus.

Paul's prayer for the Ephesians

The letter contains the following prayer. It is the prayer of a Christian teacher who is passionate to share his faith and bring to others the joy he has experienced.

I ask God from the wealth of his glory to give you power through his Spirit to be strong in your inner selves, and I pray that Christ will make his home in your hearts through faith. I pray that you may have your roots and foundation in love, so that you, together with all God's people, may have the power to understand how broad and long, how high and deep, is Christ's love. Yes, may you come to know his love – although it can never be fully known – and so be completely filled with the very nature of God.

Ephesians 3:16–19

PHILIPPIANS

The church in Philippi was one that had been set up by Paul on his second missionary journey. He went there not long after he had met a young Christian by the name of Timothy in Lystra. Paul chose him as a companion and helper (Acts 16:1–5).

Paul spreads the message

Philippi was a large Roman town in the province of Macedonia – the first church Paul actually set up in Europe. The Jews there had no synagogue but rather met by the river. There Paul and his companions met some women, who listened to his message. A wealthy cloth merchant named Lydia was so impressed with the message about Jesus she asked to be baptized at once.

Paul's arrest

Some time after, Paul healed a servant girl whose mental state meant that her owners put her to work as a fortune-teller. They were so angry that she was no longer saleable as a fortune-teller that they had Paul thrown into prison without a proper trial. As a result of all that happened, the jailer was converted to Christianity and the town officials had to apologize for their actions!

In Acts 16, Luke gives an account of Paul's imprisonment while in Philippi. Paul wrote his letter to the Philippians when he was enduring another spell of imprisonment and awaiting his sentence.

How a church meeting may have taken place. It would normally have been in the home, and all members of the household would have attended.

A joyful letter

Paul writes to Philippi from house arrest in Rome, awaiting trial. Even so, his letter is full of joy. He reminds the Philippians that their relationship with God is because of their faith in Christ.

"Don't worry about anything," he tells them, "but in all your prayers ask God for what you need, always asking him with a thankful heart. And God's peace, which is far beyond human understanding, will keep your hearts and minds safe in union with Christ Jesus" (Philippians 4:6–7).

He goes on to offer this encouragement:

… my friends, fill your minds with those things that are good and that deserve praise: things that are true, noble, right, pure, lovely, and honourable.

Philippians 4:8

The ruins of the Via Egnatia (the Egnatian Way), Philippi, which passed through the central market and forum (ruins of the forum can be seen here). Paul would have walked on this road on his way to Thessalonica from Neapolis.

COLOSSIANS

The town of Colossae lay to the east of Ephesus. Paul himself did not go there, but believers from the church he set up in Ephesus did, and they in turn preached the news about Jesus and set up a group of believers.

When Paul was living under house arrest in Rome he heard troubling news. Preachers had confused the believers in Colossae with false teachings and new rules. They were being urged to follow some of the Jewish traditions and some mysterious practices such as worshipping angels (Colossians 2:18–19).

Paul was clear: the only thing required to be friends with God was faith in Christ. Because of faith, God's Spirit would transform believers and make them new people.

The people of God

Paul describes to the Colossians the life of a Christian who is changed from within:

You are the people of God; he loved you and chose you for his own. So then, you must clothe yourselves with compassion, kindness, humility, gentleness, and patience. Be tolerant with one another and forgive one another whenever any of you has a complaint against someone else. You must forgive one another just as the Lord has forgiven you. And to all these qualities add love, which binds all things together in perfect unity.

Colossians 3:12–14

Letter exchange

Paul tells the Colossians that he has written another letter to the nearby church in Laodicea. He has the Colossians make sure they have their letter read aloud in Laodicea and also have the letter to Laodicea read in Colossae (Colossians 4:15–16).

At a church meeting, a child reads aloud from what was to become the New Testament.

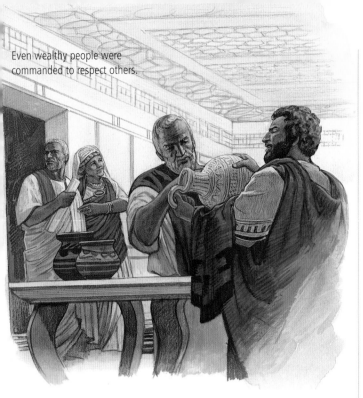

Even wealthy people were commanded to respect others.

People in the church should treat one another in this loving and respectful way. So should husbands and wives, parents and children, slaves and their masters.

Slaves and masters

The issue of slaves and masters was particularly important. Paul was also returning a runaway slave he had met in Rome to his master in Colossae. Paul had chosen Tychicus to carry his main letter, and the messenger and the runaway slave, Onesimus, were travelling together.

In this Roman stone stele, a master frees his slave. The slave touches his master's hand in the presence of a witness.

PHILEMON

Onesimus was bringing a letter especially for the master he had deserted: Philemon.

Paul's letter to Philemon is also included in the New Testament. Paul explains to Philemon that his runaway slave, Onesimus, came to Rome. There he both met Paul and became a Christian. He has proved a great help to Paul, but now it is right for him to go back to his master.

The slave Onesimus may have worn a slave badge similar to that above, which reads: "Seize me, if I should escape, and send me back to my master."

Paul explains that he wants Philemon to welcome him as a brother in Christ. Paul writes to Philemon:

Your love, dear brother, has brought me great joy and much encouragement! You have cheered the hearts of all God's people.
Verse 7

1 & 2 THESSALONIANS

Thessalonica was in the province of Macedonia (as was Philippi). Paul reached there with Silas on his second missionary journey. He went and preached in the synagogue, and his message was heard by Jews as well as Gentiles who were also attracted by the Jewish faith, and were known as "God-fearers".

Many of the people believed, but some of the Jews were angry and jealous. They complained to the local governor that Paul was telling people that Jesus was a rival king to the emperor. This proved so troublesome that Paul and Silas quickly moved on to Athens and Corinth (Acts 17).

When visiting Athens, Paul and Silas would have preached under the shadow of the Parthenon, a marble temple that still stands on the acropolis today.

Silas

Silas accompanied Paul on his first and second missionary journeys. He was briefly imprisoned with Paul when they were in Philippi, where an earthquake broke their chains and opened the prison door. Silas is often portrayed carrying broken chains.

In Athens, Paul was shocked and saddened by the extent of the idolatry he found there. As a result, he spoke to Jews and Gentiles alike about Jesus' message.

The first letter

In his letter, Paul explains why he had to leave Thessalonica so quickly. He says he was worried that the new believers had not been given enough good teaching about their new faith. So he sent an up-and-coming young missionary named Timothy to work among them (1 Thessalonians 3:2). Timothy had returned with encouraging news about their faith and their love.

Paul has also heard that they are worried about when Jesus will return, and what will happen to anyone who dies while waiting for him. He tells them not to fret: alive or dead, the believers will one day live safely with Jesus (1 Thessalonians 4:13–17).

Christian living

Paul reminds his readers of how they should live their lives now they are friends with God:

… warn the idle, encourage the timid, help the weak, be patient with everyone. See that no one pays back wrong for wrong, but at all times make it your aim to do good to one another and to all people. Be joyful always, pray at all times, be thankful in all circumstances. This is what God wants from you in your life in union with Christ Jesus.

1 Thessalonians 5:14–18

Timothy

Timothy was another trusted companion of Paul. He accompanied him on his second missionary journey, and, like Silas, was also imprisoned with Paul on one occasion.

The second letter

In his second letter to Christians in Thessalonica, Paul gives even more reassurance about "the end times". Some people have been claiming that "the day of the Lord" has already come. Not so, says Paul. There is to be a time when wickedness itself will claim to be God. Only then will Jesus come and claim his kingdom.

Romans 16:3–4

Paul's profession had been in tentmaking (1 Thessalonians 2:9; 2 Thessalonians 3:8) – just like that of missionaries Priscilla and Aquila whom he had met in Corinth (Acts 18:2–13) and with whom he had lived for eighteen months. When not preaching the word of God, Paul would ensure that he was kept busy with his craft – hence his words in 2 Thessalonians 3:11–12: "… we hear that there are some people among you who live lazy lives and who do nothing except meddle in other people's business. In the name of the Lord Jesus Christ we command these people and warn them to lead orderly lives and work to earn their own living."

1 TIMOTHY

Timothy was a young Christian from the town of Lystra in Galatia. His mother, Eunice, was a Jewish believer and his father was Greek. Paul was very impressed with Timothy's faith and understanding, and asked him to join him on his missionary journey (Acts 16:1–5).

Timothy continued to travel the empire for the sake of Christianity even after Paul was arrested and taken to stand trial in Rome. In fact, it was from Rome that Paul wrote the two letters to Timothy that are included in the New Testament.

1 and 2 Timothy, Titus, and Philemon are the only letters that are addressed to individuals, rather than whole congregations. See 1 Timothy 1:2: "To Timothy, my true son in the faith."

False teaching

Paul warns Timothy about the false teachings that have sprung up in the church. He wants Timothy to be clear about one thing: that friendship with God depends on faith in Jesus and nothing else.

This is a true saying, to be completely accepted and believed: Christ Jesus came into the world to save sinners.

1 Timothy 1:15

As a boy, Timothy was schooled according to Jewish custom by his mother, Eunice, and grandmother, Lois. When they met when Paul arrived in Lystra, Paul was impressed with Timothy's understanding, and soon converted them to Christianity.

How to lead a church

Paul also gives Timothy advice on what to include in a worship service in the church. He reminds him that a church leader must live a good life that everyone and anyone can respect. Even though Timothy is a young man, says Paul, he needs to both show respect and live a life worthy of respect (1 Timothy 3).

True riches

Paul warns Timothy about those who use religion as a way to get rich. True riches are quite different from wealth in this world. "The love of money is a source of all kinds of evil," he warns. "… But you, man of God… Strive for righteousness, godliness, faith, love, endurance, and gentleness" (1 Timothy 6:10–11).

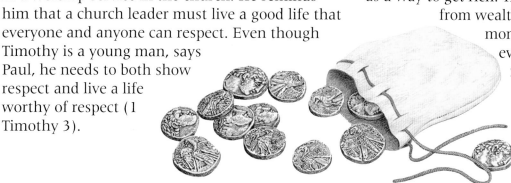
A purse containing Roman money.

2 TIMOTHY

In his second letter to Timothy, Paul talks wearily of his imprisonment and his disappointment that some whom he considered friends have deserted him. Even so, he remains confident in his faith and encourages Timothy to carry on the work of spreading the news about Jesus. He also says that he hopes Timothy will have the opportunity to visit him in Rome and bring him some books he left behind on his travels, and his coat.

Knowing the Bible

Paul remembers happily the Christian home in which Timothy was raised: his mother, Eunice, and his grandmother, Lois, were both believers. They clearly helped him to read the Bible.

… ever since you were a child, you have known the Holy Scriptures, which are able to give you the wisdom that leads to salvation through faith in Christ Jesus. All Scripture is inspired by God and is useful for teaching the truth, rebuking error, correcting faults, and giving instruction for right living, so that the person who serves God may be fully qualified and equipped to do every kind of good deed.

2 Timothy 3:15–17

From scrolls to codices

It was the Romans who invented the "codex" (manuscripts written on parchment that were bound together) replacing the scrolls of Judaism, and developing over the next 400 years or so. In the first century, at the time of Paul, the codices were in their early development, and it is important to note that in 2 Timothy 4:13, Paul asks Timothy to bring him "the books too, and especially the ones made of parchment."

One of the earliest known examples of a codex is the fragment of a page of a book, written on both sides, known as "P52" (below). P52 is housed in the John Rylands Library in Manchester, UK, and contains the handwritten text of John 18:31–33, 37, 38. It is dated between 117 and 138 CE, when books were still in their early development.

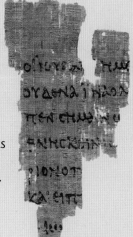

TITUS

This letter is addressed to Titus, Paul's "true son in the faith that we have in common" (1:4).

Titus was one of the people who travelled with Paul on his third missionary journey. Paul says that he left Titus in Crete so that he could make sure this new church was functioning properly.

This letter, written to strengthen and encourage Titus, provides clear instructions about the duties of those who hold positions of responsibility within the church.

Travelling by boat on the Mediterranean in Paul's time could be a dangerous business: during the months of November to March the waters were essentially closed due to the bad weather, which would include violent storms. It was this sea that Titus and Paul would have crossed to get to Crete.

The mark of a church leader

Paul reminds Titus that as a church leader he must be "self-controlled, upright, holy, and disciplined" (Titus 1:8). He must be wise enough to stop incorrect teaching creeping in, especially by those who wanted new Christians to adopt Jewish practices. It is faith in Christ that makes people God's friends.

Paul tells Titus that his teaching is not just about what to believe. Men and women, young and old, need to learn from him how to live lives that are worthy of their new faith.

… God has revealed his grace for the salvation of all people. That grace instructs us to give up ungodly living and worldly passions, and to live self-controlled, upright, and godly lives in this world, as we wait for the blessed Day we hope for, when the glory of our great God and Saviour Jesus Christ will appear.

Titus 2:11–13

PHILEMON

Titus in Corinth

Paul also talks about Titus in one of his letters to the Corinthians. Titus had rejoined Paul from a time spent in Corinth to help sort out some of the problems in the church there. It seems that Paul thought him to be a wise and effective leader.

2 Corinthians 7

In the New Testament the very short book of Philemon is included at this point. It is a letter addressed to a member of the church in Colossae. Read about the letters to the Colossians and to Philemon on pages 128–29.

Trouble ahead for Paul

Paul writes to Titus from Rome, perhaps around 68 CE. Paul's time under arrest is dragging on. It is likely that he was put to death for his faith not long after, as the Roman authorities turned against Christians.

One of the most popular forms of entertainment in Roman times was chariot-racing. Chariots would usually be pulled by four horses and each race, consisting of between four and six chariots, lasted for around seven laps of the stadium (or just over 8km). The races were held at the Circus Maximus, a stadium that could seat up to 250,000 spectators. Charioteers were usually slaves; sometimes very successful ones could become very rich.

LETTER TO THE HEBREWS

"Hebrews" is one of the words used in the Bible to refer to Jews. This letter is written to help Jewish Christians understand the relationship between their Jewish traditions and their Christian faith.

No one knows for sure who wrote this letter, but it was clearly a Christian who had a deep knowledge of the Jewish faith. One suggestion is Paul's first companion, Barnabas.

Scapegoat

A goat used in the ritual of Yom Kippur (Leviticus 16:8–10) which was symbolically laden by the high priest with the sins of the Israelites and sent into the wilderness to be destroyed.

Promise to Abraham

The letter recalls the promises made to Abraham: that his people would be God's people. Among Abraham's descendants was Moses, who brought the people laws to live by. Moses' brother Aaron became the high priest, conducting the worship services that brought the people close to God. The law and worship led by priests in the tabernacle were part of the old covenant with God.

The Old Testament practice relating to the scapegoat that is noted on the left is depicted in the vivid picture below. Jesus was thought to be the ultimate high priest and scapegoat – taking on, in his death, the blame of others – and a fulfilment of the Old Testament (Hebrews 4:14).

Jesus, the high priest

Even so, says the letter, there was already a more important priest. Melchizedek was a priest who came and met Abraham and gave him God's blessing. The writer says that Jesus is a priest of the order of Melchizedek – the high priest who brings his followers God's blessing.

All the great people of the Old Testament had faith. It was always more important than the laws about how to live and how to worship. Now those laws are replaced by faith in Jesus, the high priest of all believers.

Let us keep our eyes fixed on Jesus, on whom our faith depends from beginning to end.

Hebrews 12:2

Once again, however, faith must lead to practical change.

Try to be at peace with everyone, and try to live a holy life, because no one will see the Lord without it.

Hebrews 12:14

In 20 BCE Herod set about rebuilding the Temple. Finally completed in 64 CE it was built on a grand scale. The outer courtyard was known as the Court of the Gentiles, where many business transactions took place. Gentiles, however, could go no further into the Temple – only Jews could access the other areas. There were notices put up that said anyone who ignored this ruling would face death. It is to this separation, this dividing wall, that Paul refers in Ephesians 2:14 – that Jesus "has brought us peace by making Jews and Gentiles one people. With his own body he broke down the wall that separated them and kept them enemies."

Jewish traditions and the Christian faith

Jewish people had grown up with their traditions and felt happy keeping them even when they became believers in Jesus.

Gentile Christians who had been convinced by the teaching that they were saved by faith were puzzled and upset at the idea of having to follow Jewish rules. Paul talked about this problem in his letters, to reassure Gentiles.

When Paul went back to Jerusalem, Jewish Christians pleaded with him to make a public display of his Jewish practices, to reassure Jewish Christians (Acts 21).

As he tried to do so, some people thought he had brought Gentiles into the part of the Temple set aside for Jews. This led to uproar, and in the end, to Paul's arrest (Acts 21:27–36).

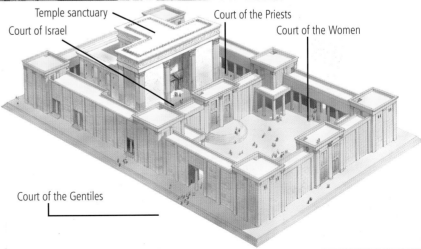

Temple sanctuary

Court of Israel

Court of the Priests

Court of the Women

Court of the Gentiles

JAMES

This is a letter written for "all God's people scattered over the whole world" (James 1:1).

The book of Acts describes the time when God's people were first scattered. Peter and other apostles had preached about Jesus and their words won them many believers. The religious authorities were anxious about this new church and made life difficult for the apostles. Still the church kept growing. Then they put a young Christian named Stephen on trial (Acts 7). He spoke wisely in defence of his faith and they had no answer. Instead, they stoned him to death – something that Paul (then Saul) watched and approved (see page 113).

Other Christians decided it was too difficult to stay in Jerusalem and they went to other Jewish communities in the surrounding provinces of Judea and Samaria (Acts 8).

Practical Christianity

The book of James is full of practical advice about how to live as a Christian and it reminds its readers not to be upset or discouraged by the difficulties they face.

In Acts 10:9–16, Peter has a vivid vision of various clean and unclean animals being lowered down on a sheet. Up until this point, the gospel has been aimed at Jews, Jewish converts and Samaritans; now it is clear that the message is for everyone – emphasized in the instruction in the vision that Peter must ignore the Jewish food rules. This clearly fits in with James' theme about the gospel being shared around the world, and with all nations (see also Romans 10:12 and Galatians 3:28).

Faith and actions

The letter openly discusses the balance between faith and actions. They must work together.

My friends, what good is it for one of you to say that you have faith if your actions do not prove it?... Show me how anyone can have faith without actions. I will show you my faith by my actions.

James 2:14, 18

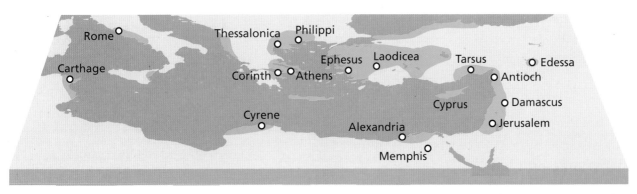

Map showing the spread of Christianity by 100 CE. God's people had indeed been "scattered over the whole world".

The Christian life

Those who have faith should show it by leading good and holy lives. They should care for and respect the poor and not treat rich people more favourably. They should control the things they say. They should treat everyone fairly and not be lured away by the desire to get wealthy. They must wait patiently for the time when Jesus returns.

The wisdom from above is pure first of all; it is also peaceful, gentle, and friendly; it is full of compassion and produces a harvest of good deeds; it is free from prejudice and hypocrisy.

James 3:17

James and the Sermon on the Mount

There are striking similarities between this letter and Jesus' teaching in the Sermon on the Mount. For example, the poor inheriting the kingdom of God (James 2:5); peacemakers are to be blessed (3:18); do not judge others (4:11–12).

Matthew 5–7

James 2:1–4 states: "… you must never treat people in different ways according to their outward appearance… If you show more respect to the well-dressed man and say to him, 'Have this best seat here,' but say to the poor man, 'Stand over there, or sit here on the floor by my feet,' then you are guilty of creating distinctions among yourselves and of making judgments based on evil motives."

1 PETER

This letter is thought by many to be the work of Jesus' own disciple Simon Peter. He was an ordinary fisherman when Jesus called him to be one of his followers, so it is not surprising that he asked for another Christian, Silas, to help him write down what he wanted to say (1 Peter 5:12).

Be strong, keep going

The letter is written to churches in five provinces of Asia: Pontus, Galatia, Cappadocia, Asia, and Bithynia. Peter reminds his readers of the hope they have in Christ. At the time of his writing in 64 CE, the Christian faith was regarded with suspicion by the Roman rulers of the empire. As a result, Christians were beginning to be persecuted.

Peter reminds them to be strong in their faith and utterly committed to living holy lives as God requires.

Who is the author?

This letter declares itself to be from Peter, but from the early years of Christianity that claim has been questioned. This is the case even though the writer declares that he was an eyewitness to events in Jesus' life (2 Peter 1:15–18). It is quite possible it was written by someone else as a tribute to Peter's teaching and authority.

Peter and the church

The Gospel of Matthew describes a conversation between Jesus and Simon Peter, in which Jesus is clearly pleased with Peter's confident faith in him. It is because Jesus regards him as his "rock" that he nicknames him "Peter" – which means rock! (See Matthew 16:13–19.)

Peter: [says Jesus] you are a rock, and on this rock foundation I will build my church, and not even death will ever be able to overcome it.

Matthew 16:18

… you are the chosen race, the King's priests, the holy nation, God's own people, chosen to proclaim the wonderful acts of God, who called you out of darkness into his own marvellous light. At one time you were not God's people, but now you are his people; at one time you did not know God's mercy, but now you have received his mercy.

1 Peter 2:9–10

As followers of Christ they are to live humble, law-abiding lives that everyone can respect. Servants are to respect their masters. Husbands and wives are to show respect and kindness to one another. Elders of the church are to serve their flock humbly.

Thrown to the lions

It seems that Peter wrote this letter from Rome. The threat of being executed for his faith was very real. He writes this to encourage his readers:

Be alert, be on watch! Your enemy, the Devil, roams around like a roaring lion, looking for someone to devour. Be firm in your faith and resist him, because you know that other believers in all the world are going through the same kind of sufferings.

1 Peter 5:8–9

2 PETER

The second letter is written to Christians everywhere. It begins with a clear call to faithful and holy living:

… do your best to add goodness to your faith; to your goodness add knowledge; to your knowledge add self-control; to your self-control add endurance; to your endurance add godliness; to your godliness add Christian affection; and to your Christian affection add love.

2 Peter 1:5–7

False teachers

The writer is concerned that people whose teaching is false have been causing havoc among the new churches. Christians are encouraged to stay true to the message they received in the beginning and that Paul has explained in his letters (2 Peter 3:16). The false teachers will reap the consequences of their wrongdoing. Those who are faithful to God will be ready for "the day of the Lord" – that will be the time when Jesus comes to claim his kingdom.

… we wait for what God has promised: new heavens and a new earth, where righteousness will be at home.

2 Peter 3:13

Left: The fear of being persecuted for Christian belief in the Roman empire was prevalent. It was not beyond the realms of possibility that a believer could be thrown to the lions.

1, 2, & 3 JOHN

These letters claim to be from Jesus' disciple John. The writer does not give a name in the first letter and the second two announce themselves simply as being from "the Elder".

1 John

The first letter reminds its readers that God is the source of true light and the giver of eternal life (1 John 1).

> *I am writing this to you so that you may know that you have eternal life – you that believe in the Son of God.*
>
> **1 John 5:13**

Jesus has enabled those who believe in him to enjoy this light and life and they should live lives of shining goodness. The Holy Spirit strengthens all believers to do so. Their call is to love God and to turn away from the false pleasures of the world.

Love

God is love, declares the writer, and so Christians must love one another.

> *Dear friends, let us love one another, because love comes from God. Whoever loves is a child of God and knows God. Whoever does not love does not know God, for God is love. And God showed his love for us by sending his only Son into the world, so that we might have life through him. This is what love is: it is not that we have loved God, but that he loved us and sent his Son to be the means by which our sins are forgiven.*
>
> **1 John 4:7–10**

> *We know that no children of God keep on sinning, for the Son of God keeps them safe, and the Evil One cannot harm them.*
>
> **1 John 5:18**

Children playing in springtime in Galilee. In John's letters, the author refers to believers – to Christians – as "my children" because they are the "children of God" who are sinless. As Jesus says in Matthew 19:14, "Let the children come to me… because the Kingdom of heaven belongs to such as these."

Right beliefs

The writer reminds his readers that they should beware of false teaching. They need to be confident in their faith and truly believe that Jesus is the Christ, the messiah.

2 John

This short letter briefly restates the themes of the first.

Christians must love one another. They must pay no attention to believers who teach wrong things about Jesus.

The writer ends by saying he hopes to visit and talk to his readers in person.

3 John

This letter is written to a church leader named Gaius. It praises him for the way he has been a great help within the church and shown love to all. The writer warns about the teaching of someone named Diotrephes and adds:

My dear friend, do not imitate what is bad but imitate what is good. Whoever does good belongs to God; whoever does what is bad has not seen God.

3 John:11

JUDE

This letter is very like 2 Peter and may have been written around the same time.

It expresses grave concern about false teachers. They have twisted the message about Jesus and use sly arguments to justify their wrongdoing.

Wild waves of the sea

They will reap the consequences of their wrongdoing. Christians are to stay true to the teaching of the apostles so they will be ready to take their place in God's presence.

Those who have gone astray are likened to "trees that bear no fruit, even in autumn" (verse 12) or "wild waves of the sea" (verse 13).

REVELATION

The book of Revelation announces itself as the work of John. According to ancient tradition this is the apostle John. It is around 95 CE, and the writer is living in exile on the Greek island of Patmos. Roman emperors have been increasingly hostile to Christians.

The book begins with a clear vision of Christ, who tells John what to put in his book.

The four horsemen of the apocalypse each riding on a different coloured horse: white symbolizing conquest, red for war, black for famine, and the pale one symbolizing death.

Visions

Revelation contains many extraordinary visions. Here are some that have become well known in general culture.

War in heaven

A war breaks out in heaven, in which Michael and heaven's angels fight against the dragon and his angels. The dragon is described as "that ancient serpent, named the Devil, or Satan, that deceived the whole world" (Revelation 12:7–9).

Four horsemen of the apocalypse

Four riders each on a different coloured horse symbolize the disasters that will come before God's rule is established: conquest, war, famine, and death (Revelation 6:1–8).

The heavenly city

The description of the heavenly city and the gates of pearl (pearly gates) has shaped many people's idea of what heaven is like (Revelation 21, especially verse 21).

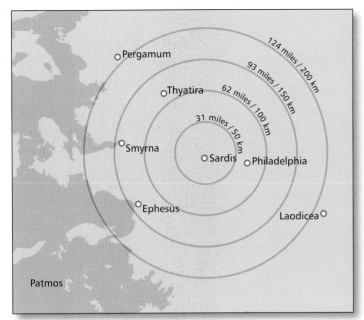

Map showing the seven churches named in Revelation.

An artist imagines how the "new heaven" mentioned in Revelation might look.

Seven churches

There are special messages to churches in seven cities in the Roman province of Asia: Ephesus, Smyrna, Pergamum, Thyatira, Sardis, Philadelphia, and Laodicea. Each of the seven messages is different but each in its own way urges church members to be more committed and more courageous in troubled times.

The Apocalypse

The book of Revelation is also known as the Apocalypse. Since the time of Daniel several works of this type had been written. Each claimed to be a vision of the heavenly realms and attempted to provide a glimpse of God's eternal plans. This type of writing was treasured by the Jews during the long years in which they were a defeated nation, ruled by foreigners. One day, the writings claimed, God would act to put right all that was wrong.

For Christians, the key act of God was to send Jesus to enable all people to live as God's people for ever.

A vision of heaven

From chapter 4 onwards the book provides glimpses of heaven and of the mighty battles that will take place between the forces of evil and the forces of good.

In the end, the forces of good win a complete victory. The writer describes "a new heaven and a new earth" (Revelation 21:1).

A voice speaks from a heavenly throne:

Now God's home is with people! He will live with them, and they shall be his people. God himself will be with them, and he will be their God. He will wipe away all tears from their eyes. There will be no more death, no more grief or crying or pain. The old things have disappeared.

Revelation 21:3–4

Finally, Jesus announces that he himself is "coming soon".

I will bring my rewards with me, to give to each one according to what he has done. I am the first and the last, the beginning and the end.

Revelation 22:12–13

THE CHRISTIAN BIBLE

Jesus was a Jew who knew and loved the Scriptures of his faith. His first followers were Jewish too, and they shared the same traditions.

When non-Jews – Gentiles – became Christians, they also wanted to know and understand the Scriptures that Jesus had so often referred to.

These early Christians often used the Greek translation of the Hebrew Bible, the Septuagint (see pages 90–91).

Writings of the first Christians

At first, the news about Jesus was preached: taught aloud. Soon the number of Christians grew so much that people who had actually known Jesus could never ever reach them. Also the places where there were churches became more widespread. It became useful for Christians to write down what they knew.

Some wrote accounts of Jesus' life, the Gospels (see pages 96–97).

Others wrote letters to individual Christians and to churches – and, indeed, to the Christian community at large.

These documents were greatly respected. They were shared and copied.

The first collection

An old tradition says that Paul's letters were the first of these Christian writings to be gathered together. It claims that Onesimus, the runaway slave whom Paul returned to Philemon (see page 129), became bishop of Ephesus. He saw it as his duty to make sure that the teachings of Paul, whom he had served in life, were kept safe for all Christians.

Which books to choose?

In the century of the time of Jesus many people wrote about their new faith. There were several accounts of Jesus' life and many letters and other writings in which Christians gave their view of what it meant to follow him.

Unsurprisingly, arguments arose about which of the writings could really be trusted and which were misleading or downright wrong.

The great councils

In 363 CE there was an important council of church leaders in Laodicea. It produced a list, or canon, of the books that they thought fit to include as Scripture. Another similar meeting was held in Carthage in 397 CE and it revised the list. The result was a canon of Scripture, a Bible, that included the books of the Jewish faith that had been translated and included in the Septuagint (pages 90–91) and the New Testament books included in Bibles to this day (for a full list, see page 159).

These books, and these books alone, were authorized to be read in churches around the empire.

Early church councils

Throughout the period of the early church, various councils of church leaders (like the one at Laodicea) met to discuss the controversies of the day and to establish the doctrine of the Christian church.

One of the most well-known councils was the one that met in Nicea in 325 CE. From this they declared a man called Arius a heretic (that is, someone who holds different views to the church about Jesus) and also formulated what we now know as the "Nicene Creed", which is still used in church services today.

Stories of Jesus' birth

The story of Jesus' birth is told and retold at Christmas to this day. This is the nativity story – the word "nativity" simply means "birth". It is drawn from the accounts in the canonical Gospels of Matthew and Luke.

In the second century CE there was great enthusiasm for more details about Jesus' birth, and that of his mother, Mary, and wider family. There are several so-called "infancy gospels" that date from this time. Some of the details in them have passed into tradition – such as the idea that Mary's mother was named Anna, and that Joseph was a widower who had children from his first marriage.

Bishops gather in Nicea (modern-day Iznik, in Turkey) to discuss the issues of the day. Arius is seen in the foreground of the picture.

Mary and Joseph set out for Bethlehem.

TRANSLATING THE BIBLE

The first translation of the Jewish Scriptures was from Hebrew to Greek because it had become the common language of the Greek empire. It continued to remain the common language of the Roman empire, although the language of the Romans – Latin – became the language of government.

The books that became the New Testament were written in Greek and for many years they were copied and recopied only in Greek.

Official religion

For the first centuries of the faith Christianity was viewed with suspicion by the Roman authorities and sometimes actively persecuted. However, in 312 CE Emperor Constantine dramatically changed his views and in the following year passed a law that made Christianity an approved faith. After his time, in 380 CE, Christianity was made the official religion of the Roman empire.

The Vulgate

From the time of Constantine onward there was a drive to produce translations in Latin, and several were made. In 384 CE Pope Damasus decided it was time to have one official Latin translation of the entire Bible. He gave the task to his secretary, a scholar named Jerome.

Jerome made a fresh translation of the Hebrew Scriptures from the Hebrew itself and also translated the Greek texts into Latin. The result was called the *versio vulgata*, meaning version commonly used. This became shortened to *vulgata*, and is referred to today as the Vulgate.

Jesus' own words

Jesus lived in the time of the Roman empire and it is likely he knew four languages: Aramaic, the spoken language of everyday in his region; Hebrew, for reading the Jewish scriptures; Greek; and Latin. In the Gospels are just a scattering of Aramaic phrases to indicate the very words Jesus would have said aloud.

Talitha, koum: "Little girl, I tell you to get up!", Mark 5:41 (Jesus' words to Jairus' daughter to raise her from death).

Abba: "Father", Mark 14:36, NIV (how Jesus addressed God in prayer as his crucifixion approaches).

Eloi, Eloi, lema sabachthani?: "My God, my God, why did you abandon me?", Mark 15:34 (words of Jesus from the cross, quoting Psalm 22).

Above: A bust of the Roman emperor Constantine I.

Above right: An ornate page from a twelfth-century copy of the Vulgate.

Other languages

The Bible was also translated into other languages in the early centuries of Christianity.

One was Syriac, a variant of Aramaic spoken in Syria. The translation is known as the Peshitta (meaning "pure") and is still used by Christians from Syria through to India.

Coptic is a language that comes from ancient Egyptian. A translation into Coptic was begun in the third century. The Coptic translation is still used in Coptic churches in North West Africa.

As the church began to spread beyond the bounds of the old Roman empire, more translations into local languages were made. Among the most significant was the translation into Slavonic. A version of the Slavonic translation is used by the Russian Orthodox church to this day.

In the ninth century, Cyril and Methodius developed the Slavonic language so that the Slavic people could have access to a Bible in their own language.

An early manuscript of the Gospel of Luke written in Coptic.

As the message of Christianity, which was now the official religion of the Roman empire, travelled around the world, more churches began to be established for the local community. This is how the fourth-century church at the Roman town of Silchester in England may have looked at the time.

149

TELLING THE BIBLE

In today's world copies of books are quickly and easily available in paper and electronic form. Many people are able to access them and also to read them for themselves.

When the earliest of the Bible books were written, they were painstakingly copied by hand. Rewriting by hand remained the only way of making copies for many centuries.

In that time, learning to read was also for the few. People who wanted to learn about their faith and to pass it on to others had to find ways to share what the Bible said.

Public occasions

In the Old Testament are examples of the Scriptures being read aloud to the people at important gatherings. Leaders of the nations who wanted people to be faithful to God's laws simply read them aloud. King Josiah ordered such a reading (2 Kings 23:2) and so did Ezra (Nehemiah 8:1–12).

The prophets too often preached their message aloud. Jeremiah felt very troubled when he was forbidden to do so and asked his scribe Baruch to write down his message and read it in the temple when a religious event meant it would be full of worshippers.

"You are to read the scroll aloud," [Jeremiah told Baruch,] "so that they will hear everything that the Lord has said to me and that I have dictated to you. Do this where everyone can hear you, including the people of Judah who have come in from their towns. Perhaps they will pray to the Lord and turn from their evil ways, because the Lord has threatened this people with his terrible anger and fury."

Jeremiah 36:6–7

One of the best preserved synagogues is that in Capernaum, an ancient fishing village situated on Lake Galilee, where Jesus lived for a time during his Galilean ministry (Matthew 4:13) and also where Peter lived (Matthew 8:14). It is here in Capernaum that Jesus healed the servant of the centurion (in fact the centurion was credited with building the synagogue – see Luke 7:5). Although it dates from around the fourth century, existing walls from another synagogue, from the time of Jesus, have been found to have been used as part of the walls of the current synagogue.

Synagogues and schools

From the time of the exile the Jews set up meeting places – synagogues – where teachers, known as rabbis, could explain the faith. Each synagogue wanted to have its own collection of Scriptures and these were treasured.

Synagogue schools were often set up next to the synagogue. Here young boys would be taught to read and write. That way they would be able to take their turn reading aloud from the Scriptures to the rest of the community. Jesus took his turn in this way (see pages 64–65 on Isaiah 56–65, and Luke 4:16–19).

The apostle Paul was a scholar of the Jewish faith and was often invited to speak in the local synagogue on his travels. He took the opportunity to explain his belief that in Jesus the old Scriptures had come true.

An example of Bible stories being told through stained glass windows. This scene is of the miraculous catch of fish, a story told in Luke's Gospel.

Preaching and teaching

Jesus himself had preached his message wherever he could gather a crowd: in the synagogue, in the Temple, by Lake Galilee, or wherever there was space outdoors. His followers did the same as they began to spread the message about him.

As Christians began to meet in churches they were eager to have written accounts of the life of Jesus and letters from the apostles. When these books were gathered together into the Bible and churches began to have their own buildings, it became customary always to have a reading or several readings from the Bible.

The Bible retold

Over the centuries, Christians found other ways to pass on the message of the Bible. Its stories became the subject of church art, including wall paintings and stained glass windows. From the Middle Ages the stories might be acted out in open-air productions, often performed from wagons. Such "mystery plays" had enduring appeal, and the tradition has been revived in modern times.

A medieval mystery play depicting the nativity scene takes place in front of large crowds. This tradition continues in some places even today.

Learning by heart

From the earliest days of humankind, many stories and sayings have been told aloud so they can be learned by heart and passed down from one generation to another. Both Jews and Christians have made a point of encouraging young people to memorize important passages from the Scriptures: various Psalms, for example, the prayer that Jesus taught (the Lord's Prayer), and the Ten Commandments.

ALL OVER THE WORLD

Up to the fifteenth century only a minority of Christians had access to a Bible – among them the church leaders and wealthy people, who could afford a handwritten copy. In Western Europe nearly every Bible copy was in Latin: the Vulgate (see page 148).

Then things changed.

Printing

In the fifteenth century craftsmen began developing a printing process that would change for ever the way copies of books were made. Tiny blocks each containing a raised letter could be assembled in the order required to make up a page of words. This printing block was then inked and stamped on paper to create a printed page. The process could be repeated over and over again, and blocks assembled for all the pages of a book.

Johann Gutenberg of Germany was among the first to experiment with the process and he had a commercial printing press from around 1450. The first book he printed – the Gutenberg Bible, a copy of the Vulgate – was printed in Germany in 1455.

As the technology developed it became easier to produce books quickly and cheaply.

A reconstruction of the Gutenberg Press, the first to utilize movable type. It revolutionized printing and enabled the written word to be accessed by many people around the world. The copying and illustrating of manuscripts began to die out as the popularity of the printing press took hold. The Gutenberg Press was the very press on which Martin Luther's writings were printed. It allowed his message of reform to reach hundreds of thousands of people.

The Reformation

In 1517 a revolution began in Christianity. A German monk named Martin Luther felt very uneasy about the Roman Catholic Church – about its teaching and its practices. He felt it was far removed from the kind of Christianity he could read about in the Bible. Famously, he nailed a list of ninety-five questions he wanted discussed to the door of his church in Wittenberg.

Left: Martin Luther.

He probably hadn't expected the extreme reaction they received. The church authorities were furious at what they saw as a dangerous challenge. Four years later, the Pope officially declared he was no longer part of the church.

Martin Luther was not cowed by this. Nor was he the only person to question the teaching of the church. More and more people began to protest about the state of the Roman Catholic Church and wanted reforms. They became known as Protestants and the movement as the Protestant Reformation.

Going back to the teachings of the Bible was very important for the Protestants. They were eager to have it translated out of Latin and into the languages that people spoke. That way, it could be read – alone or aloud – and readers and listeners would be able to understand the meaning.

Among those who wanted good translations for all was a Dutch scholar named Erasmus. He put together a version of the New Testament in Greek. He did his research carefully so as to be sure it would be a reliable version from which other translations could be made.

Exploration

From the fifteenth century onwards, Europeans began exploring the world as never before. Sea travel made it easier to reach parts of India and Asia that previously had not been accessible. Other navigators discovered the Americas and, later, Australia and other lands and civilizations in the South Pacific.

The first explorers were looking for new territories with valuable resources. Soon missionaries began travelling to these new territories, eager to spread their Christian faith. Wherever they went, they were keen to make as much as possible of the Bible available in the languages spoken.

By the end of the twentieth century, the Bible had been translated into nearly all of the world's languages.

Far left: A portrait of Erasmus.
Left: A 1520 edition of Erasmus' New Testament.

READING THE BIBLE

It is often said that the Bible is the world's best-selling book. It is certainly widely available. Over the years Bible societies have been established and funded to make sure that as many people who wish to have one can do so at little or no cost.

The question is often raised about how much it is read. As with all books, fewer people read any or all of the Bible than actually could. Even so, it is still widely read and highly valued for a variety of reasons.

A Chinese worker feeds Bible paper into a printing press. A joint venture between the Amity Foundation and the United Bible Societies, the company's priority is to print Bibles and Christian literature for the churches in China. Since 1987, the company has printed over 32 million Bibles in several languages including Braille and that of eight Chinese minority groups. The Bibles are distributed to over 50,000-odd churches and meeting places in mainland China.

An ancient book

The writings in the Bible are all at least 2,000 years old, and some are much older. They give insights into beliefs and customs from long ago. The story books give their version of events that are known to have happened and that can be compared with other writings from the past. As ancient documents, they are a treasure trove for the scholar – even one who is sceptical about matters of faith.

Insight into what people are like

In different ways the books of the Bible show what people are like: what drives them to different choices about how they should live their lives, what is considered right, and what is considered wrong for nations and for individuals. These insights provide much to reflect on for readers who are seeking answers to the same questions and problems even today.

Stories from around the world

The *Epic of Gilgamesh* is a Babylonian poem containing an account of a flood, bearing remarkable likeness to the flood story in Genesis. Altogether twelve clay tablets re-telling this ancient *Epic* have been discovered; the flood story is told in the eleventh tablet (right). These tablets were written in the Akkadian language.

The biblical story of the flood and Noah's ark is visualized in this 2010 painting.

Genesis 6:9 – 9:17

A 1925 image of God's creation, in which humankind, as the guardian of God's created world, is represented by Adam.

A transforming read

Christians claim that the Bible as a whole transforms their view of the world. It is one in which the life and words of Jesus show them what it means to live in the way that they were created for – as children of a just and loving God.

Their faith in God leads them to live in the way that Jesus taught, treating others with the generosity and justice they would expect for themselves.

Ultimate questions

The Bible is written by people who believed that a God created the universe and sets the standard for right and wrong. Reading it provides glimpses into their view of ultimate questions: why are we here?; how should we live?; what happens when we die?

INDEX

Names

A Aaron 17, 136
Abednego 72
Abraham 10, 17, 136, 137
Absalom 31
Adam and Eve 8
Ahab, King 34, 35, 40
Ahaziah, King 40
Alexander the Great 90, 94
Amos 37, 76, 77
Angel Gabriel 104
Antiochus IV Epiphanes, King 94
Artaxerxes, King 47
Ashurbanipal, King 55
Astarte (Asherah) 25, 28, 35
Athaliah 42

B Baal 25, 28, 34
Barnabas 103, 115, 122, 136
Bartimaeus 102
Bathsheba 31, 53
Belshazzar 73
Boaz 26, 27

C Cain and Abel 8
Constantine, Emperor 148
Cyril 149
Cyrus, King 45, 46, 73

D Damasus, Pope 148
Daniel 7, 72–73
Darius, Emperor 46, 49, 94
Darius the Mede 73
David, King 27–31, 44, 52, 61, 88

E Edomites 43, 77
Eli 28
Elihu 51
Elijah 34, 35
Elisha 36
Erasmus 153
Esther 48–49
Eunice 132, 133
Ezekiel 7, 70–71
Ezra 25, 44, 46, 54, 89, 150

F Fra Mauro 153

G Goliath 29
Gutenberg, Johannes 152

H Habakkuk 83, 118
Haggai 46, 85
Haman 48, 49
Hazael, King 35
Herod, King 98, 137
Hezekiah, King 37, 38, 40, 41, 44, 56, 61, 84
Hosea 37, 74

I Isaac 10
Isaiah 7, 60–65, 81

J Jacob 10, 11, 77
Jairus 103
James 138–139
Jehoiachin 43, 67
Jehoiakim 42
Jehu 35, 36, 40
Jeremiah 7, 66–68, 89, 150
Jeroboam, King 11, 37, 76
Jerome 148
Jesus 4, 20, 137
  birth 60, 104, 147
  books of life 96
  boyhood 105
  crucifixion and resurrection 103
  The Good Shepherd 62
  ministry 97
  name 22
  new Covenant 96
  Prince of Peace 86
  rededication of temple 95
  Sermon on the Mount 99
  as suffering servant 63
  at the synagogue 65
  washing of feet 110
Jethro 12, 14
Jezebel 34, 35
Joahaz, King 42
Job 50–51
Joel 75
John 142–143, 144
John the Baptist 104
Jonah 37, 78–80
Joseph, father of Jesus 105
Joseph, son of Jacob 11
Joshua 19, 22–23, 24
Josiah, King 42, 44, 83, 89, 150
Judas 111
Judas Maccabeus 94, 95
Jude 143

L Lazarus 109
Luke 112

Luther, Martin 152–153

M Malachi 87
Mark 102–103
Mary, mother of Jesus 105
Matthew 98–101
Melchizedek 137
Meshach 72
Micah 81, 98
Mordecai 48, 49
Moses 6, 12–21, 88, 136

N Naaman the Syrian 36
Nahum 82
Naomi 26, 27
Nathan 30, 31
Nebuchadnezzar, King 42, 43, 45, 46, 67, 68, 72, 73
Nehemiah 47, 75
Noah 8, 9

O Obadiah 77
Obed 27, 29
Onesimus 129, 146

P Paul (Saul)
  conversion 113
  letters 116, 118–119
  and Luke 104
  missionary work 114–115, 120–131
  on Scriptures 4, 150
  and Stephen 138
Peter (Simon Peter) 75, 111, 113, 138, 140–141
Philemon 129
Philistines 28, 29
Pontius Pilate 110
Ptolemy II Philadelphus, King 91

R Rehoboam 34
Ruth 26–27

S Samuel 27, 28–31
Satan 50, 144
Saul (New Testament) *see* Paul
Saul (Old Testament) 29
Sennacherib, King 37, 38, 41, 61
Shadrach 72
Shalmaneser III, King 36
Shalmaneser V, King 37, 41, 77
Sheba, Queen of 33
Silas 115, 130

Solomon, King 30, 33, 44, 53, 56, 58, 89
  Judgment of 32
Stephen 138

T Timothy 126, 131, 132–133
Titus 134–135
Tychicus 129

U Uriah 31, 53

X Xerxes, King 48, 49
Zechariah 46, 86
Zedekiah 43, 67
Zephaniah 83, 84

Places

A Alexandria 91, **95**, **114**
Assyria and Assyrian empire 37, 40, 42, **45**, 60, 61, **65**, 77, 78, 81–82, 84
Athens **114**, 130
Attalia **114**, 122

B Babylon 9, **10**, 33, 43, 45, 62, **65**, 67, 70, 73, 89, 90, **95**
Bethel **23**, 34
Bethlehem 26, 27, 81, 98, 104

C Caesarea **114**
Caesarea Philippi 102
Canaan **10**, 12, 15, 18–25
Capernaum 65, **97**, 150
Carthage **139**, 146
Colossae **114**, 128–129
Corinth **114**, 120–121, 130, 135
Crete **112**, 134
China 154

D Dan **23**, 34

E Egypt **10**, 11, 12–15, 18, 19, 21, **33**
Ephesus **114**, 115, 117, 124–125, 128, **139**, **145**

G Galatia 115, 122–123, 132
Gath-hepher **79**

Greek empire 90, 92, **95**, 120, 148

J Jericho 22, **23**
   Jerusalem 40–47, 62, 64, 68, 70, 71, **77**, 84–87, 98, 103, 113
   Lachish 37, 41

L Laodicea 128, **139**, **145**, 146
   Lystra **114**, 132

M Mount Nebo **19**, 21
   Mount of Beatitudes, Tabgha 99
   Mount Sinai 12, 14, 15, **19**, 20

N Nazareth 65, **77**, **97**
   Nicea 146, 147
   Nineveh **10**, 37, **45**, **65**, 78, **79**, 80, 82

P Patmos 144, **145**
   Persia and Persian empire 46, 48, 49, 94
   Philippi **114**, 126–127, 130, **139**

R River Jordan 19, **23**, 36, 97, 102, 104
   Rome and Roman empire **112**, **114**, 116–119, 120, 124, **139**, 141, 148

S Samaria **34**, 41, **45**, **65**, 106, 138
   Sea of Galilee **23**, 90, **97**, 99
   Shiloh **23**, 28, 30
   Susa 49, **95**

T Tarshish **79**
   Thessalonica **114**, 130–131, **139**

Subjects

A Angels 72, 73, 103, 104
   Apocalypse 145
   Apostles 113
   Ark of the covenant 15, 16, 28, 30, 68
   "Armour of God" 125

B Babylonian Chronicle 43
   Bible
      Christian Bible 146–147
      Old Testament 4, 6–7, 38–39, 88–89
      original manuscript 5
      reading of 133, 154–155
      as transformative 155
      translation of 148–149, 153, 154

C Census 18
   Christian living 131
   Christianity, spread of 139
   Church as body 120
   Church leaders, mark of 134
   Codex Sinaiticus 91
   Codices 133
   Church councils 146
   Covenant 9, 10, 15, 17, 23, 68, 121, 136
   Creation 8, 155
   Cyrus cylinder 45

D Day of the Lord 141
   Dead Sea Scrolls 89
   Disasters 75
   Disciples 112–115
   Disobedience 33, 34, 40, 78
   Dry bones 71

E Earning a living 131
   Eastern Orthodox Church 93
   End times (last judgment) 101, 131, 145
   Eucharist 121
   Exile 32, 43, 45, 46, 53, 62, 67, 89–90
   Exodus of Israelites 13
   Exploration 153

F Faith 128, 138
   False teachings 128, 141, 143
   Families 87
   Festivals 21
   Following Jesus 101
   Four horsemen of the apocalypse 144
   Fra Mauro Map 153
   Freedom 123

G "Garden Tomb" 103
   "Gezer Calendar" 58
   Golden calf 17, 33
   Good Samaritan 106

Good shepherd 63, 71, 86, 109
Greek language 91, 96, 148
Gutenberg Bible 152

H Hanukkah 95
   Harvest 21
   Heaven, vision of 145
   Heavenly city 144
   Holiness 18
   Holy of Holies 16, 17, 33
   Holy Spirit 105, 112, 119, 142

I "I am" 108–109
   Identity 46
   Inheritance 11
   Insight 154
   Isaiah Scroll 4, 89

J Jewish Christians 98, 136, 137

K Kindness 64
   Kingdom of heaven 100, 101

L Last supper 97, 110, 111, 120
   Latin 148
   Laws 15, 16, 20, 22, 28, 122
   Light and love 110
   Lord's Prayer 100, 105
   Lord's Supper 120, 121

M Manna 14
   Memorization 151
   Miracles 12, 13, 22, 35, 41, 72, 84, 101, 102, 108–109
   Missionary journeys 113, 114–115, 132–133
   "Mystery plays" 151

N Nativity 147, 151
   "Nicene Creed" 146

O Oxus Treasure 49

P Parables 106–107
   Passover 12, 21, 42, 55, 105
   Pentecost 21, 75, 112
   Persecution 140, 141, 148
   "Phylacteries" 20
   Plagues 12
   Practical Christianity 138–139
   Prayer 28, 31, 33, 35, 80, 100, 125

Printing 152
Prodigal Son 106
Protestant Church 92, 152
Purin, festival of 48

R Reformation 152
   Resurrection 103, 109, 111
   Riches, danger of 76, 84, 100, 133
   Roman Catholic Church 92–93, 152–153

S Scapegoats 136
   Scriptures 90–91, 150–51
   Scrolls 4, 5, 89, 92, 133
   Sermon on the Mount 99, 139
   Seven churches 145
   Shelters, festival of 21
   Slavery 11, 12, 110, 129, 135
   Song of Songs (Song of Solomon) 7, 59
   Storms 35, 70, 78, 102, 119, 134
   Storytelling 88
   Suffering 50–51
   Synagogues 65, 90, 150
   Synoptic Gospels 96–97
   Tabernacle 16, 30

T "Taylor's Prism" 61
   Ten Commandments 14, 15, 88

U Unfaithfulness to God 3, 70, 74, 81

V Visions 70, 73, 144
   Vulgate Bible 148

W War in Heaven 144
   Weddings 59
   Wilderness 14, 18
   Wisdom 56–57
   Wise men 98
   Writing on the wall 73

Y Yom Kippur 136

THE BOOKS OF THE BIBLE: QUICK FINDER

In alphabetical order

1 Chronicles	Ecclesiastes	Lamentations
1 Corinthians	Ephesians	Leviticus
1 John	Esther	Luke
1 Kings	Exodus	Malachi
1 Peter	Ezekiel	Mark
1 Samuel	Ezra	Matthew
1 Thessalonians	Galatians	Micah
1 Timothy	Genesis	Nahum
2 Chronicles	Habakkuk	Nehemiah
2 Corinthians	Haggai	Numbers
2 John	Hebrews	Obadiah
2 Kings	Hosea	Philemon
2 Peter	Isaiah	Philippians
2 Samuel	James	Proverbs
2 Thessalonians	Jeremiah	Psalms
2 Timothy	Job	Revelation
3 John	Joel	Romans
Acts (of the Apostles)	John	Ruth
Amos	Jonah	Song of Solomon
Colossians	Joshua	Titus
Daniel	Jude	Zechariah
Deuteronomy	Judges	Zephaniah

In canonical order

Old Testament

Genesis

Exodus

Leviticus

Numbers

Deuteronomy

Joshua

Judges

Ruth

1 Samuel

2 Samuel

1 Kings

2 Kings

1 Chronicles

2 Chronicles

Ezra

Nehemiah

Esther

Job

Psalms

Proverbs

Ecclesiastes

Song of Solomon

Isaiah

Jeremiah

Lamentations

Ezekiel

Daniel

Hosea

Joel

Amos

Obadiah

Jonah

Micah

Nahum

Habakkuk

Zephaniah

Haggai

Zechariah

Malachi

New Testament

Matthew

Mark

Luke

John

Acts (of the Apostles)

Romans

1 Corinthians

2 Corinthians

Galatians

Ephesians

Philippians

Colossians

1 Thessalonians

2 Thessalonians

1 Timothy

2 Timothy

Titus

Philemon

Hebrews

James

1 Peter

2 Peter

1 John

2 John

3 John

Jude

Revelation

Text by Peter Martin

This edition copyright © 2017 Lion Hudson

Published by Lion Books
an imprint of
Lion Hudson plc
Wilkinson House, Jordan Hill Road,
Oxford OX2 8DR, England
www.lionhudson.com/lionchildrens

ISBN 978 0 7459 7705 8

First edition 2017

Acknowledgments

The publishers would like to thank Miranda Lever for all her assistance with this book.

Unless otherwise stated, illustrations are by Chris Molan, copyright © 1994, 1995, 1996 Lion Hudson.

Unless otherwise marked, Scripture quotations are taken from the Good News Bible published by the Bible Societies and HarperCollins Publishers, © American Bible Society 1994, used with permission.

pp. 58, 86, 148: Scripture quotations taken from the Holy Bible, New International Version, copyright © 1973, 1978, 1984 International Bible Society. Used by permission of Hodder & Stoughton, a member of the Hodder Headline Group. All rights reserved. 'NIV' is a trademark of International Bible Society. UK trademark number 1448790.

A catalogue record for this book is available from the British Library

Printed and bound in China, January 2017, LH41

Picture Acknowledgments

t=top, b=bottom, c=centre, l=left, r=right

Alamy: pp. 35tr/www.BibleLandPictures.com, 36tr/www.BibleLandPictures.com, 54tc/Ryan Rodrick Beiler, 55tl/www.BibleLandPictures.com, 58t/www.BibleLandPictures.com, 61b/www.BibleLandPictures.com, 62c/Hanan Isachar, 63l/Steve Skjold, 71b/PhotoStock-Israel, 73t/1 Collection, 74t/Ivan Vdovin, 75r/epa european pressphoto agency b.v., 78b/nik wheeler, 81b/Everett Collection Historical, 83b/Espiocs, 84b/www.BibleLandPictures.com, 86b/Hanan Isachar, 90tl/www.BibleLandPictures.com, 90bl/www.BibleLandPictures.com, 91tr/www.BibleLandPictures.com, 92b/Granger Historical Picture Archive, 93b/imageBROKER, 95tr/Panagiotis Karapanagiotis, 98b/Jon Arnold Images Ltd, 98br/www.BibleLandPictures.com, 99t/Naeblys, 108br/Heritage Image Partnership Ltd, 116br/The Art Archive, 118tr/The Art Archive, 120b/Greece, 12l/Ivan Vdovin, 125c/Brian Jannsen, 133br/www.BibleLandPictures.com, 143r/All Canada Photos, 145/GL Archive, 153bl/Prisma Archivo, 153br/WENN Ltd, 154tr/epa european pressphoto agency b.v.

AKG Images: pp. 11b/James Morris, 37r/Erich Lessing, 93tr/Zev Radovan/BibleLandPictures

Art Archive: pp. 19tr/Jane Taylor, 28tl/Israel Museum Jerusalem/Gianni Dagli Orti, 110t/DeA Picture Library/S. Vannini, 123tr/Museo della Civilta Romana Rome/Gianni Dagli Orti, 129b/Museo della Civilta Romana Rome/Gianni Dagli Orti, 148tr/Bibliotheque Municipale Interuniversitaire Clermont-Ferrand/Kharbine-Tapabor, 149tr/DeA Picture Library/W. Buss

Bible Places: pp. 5c, 15tl, 15br, 16b, 20l, 20r, 25br, 26t, 43tr, 45bl, 49tr, 62b, 89b, 98b, 103br, 109tr, 110l, 123b, 127b/Todd Bolen, 25bc, 49tr/A.D. Riddle, 27b/Craig Dunning, 46bl/Kim Guess, 150tr/Bill Schlegel

Bridgeman: pp. 5t/The Israel Museum, Jerusalem, Israel, 13tl/Werner Forman Archive, 17tl/Palazzo Ducale, Venice, Italy/Cameraphoto Arte Venezia, 38t/Chartres Cathedral, Chartres, France, 38b/McConnell, James Edwin (1903-95)/Private Collection/© Look and Learn, 39c/Brock, Henry Matthew (1875-1960)/Private Collection, 39b/Relief depicting Xerxes I (c.519-465 BCE) with two attendants (stone), Achaemenid, (550-330 BCE) / Persepolis, Iran, 41t/Israel Museum, Jerusalem, Israel, 50l/Pictures from History, 49tl/Persian School/Persepolis, Iran 71tr/Stanhope, John Roddam Spencer (1829-1908)/Private Collection/Photo © Christie's Images, 63l/ Tissot, James Jacques Joseph (1836-1902)/Brooklyn Museum of Art, New York, USA, 95t/Tristram, Professor Ernest (1892-1952 /Palace of Westminster, London, UK, 95c/Private Collection/Photo © Zev Radovan, 118b/De Agostini Picture Library/Archivio J. Lange, 137tr/Private Collection © Look and Learn, 145tr/Musee des Tapisseries, Angers, France, 148c/Louvre, Paris, France/Peter Willi, 149bl/De Agostini Picture Library/G. Dagli Orti, 151br/Petts, Kenneth John (1907-92)/Private Collection © Look and Learn, 153tr/Universal History Archive/UIG, 154br/Tattersfield, Jane/Private Collection./Private Collection/Archives Charmet, 154bl/Universal History Archive/UIG, 155c/Galleria Civica d'Arte Moderna, Milan, Italy

Chris Molan Artwork: 1c, 2c, 3r, 5b, 6b, 8br, 9c, 10b, 11t, 12bl, 13b, 14b, 17b, 18c, 21b, 22b, 23b, 24b, 25t, 26t, 27b, 28b, 29b, 30br, 32b, 33tr, 35b, 36b, 40r, 41b, 42b, 44b, 47b, 48b, 52b, 53b, 54bl, 54cr, 55br, 57c, 58b, 59b, 60b, 61t, 64b, 65b, 66tr, 67b, 68b, 69b, 70c, 72c, 74b, 76b, 79r, 80b, 82b, 85b, 87b, 88r, 90r, 91b, 94b, 96l, 99b, 100b, 101t, 102b, 104b, 106b, 109b, 110b, 111t, 112b, 113b, 113t, 115b, 117b, 119b, 121b, 122b, 124r, 126l, 127t, 128b, 129tl, 130b, 131r, 132b, 134b, 135b, 136b, 138b, 139b, 140br, 142b, 144b, 147b, 149b

David Alexander: p. 130tr

Getty Images: pp. 9l/Rodrigo Arangua/AFP, 51r/Danita Delimont, 122l/Laszlo Szirtesi, 152c/Imagno

Lion Hudson: pp. 8l, 10tr, 19l, 23tr, 30bl, 33br, 34r, 45tr, 65tr, 77c, 79r, 85b, 95b, 97l, 97r, 103t, 108t, 112r, 114c, 121c, 129tr, 137br, 139t, 145tl

Rex Nicholls: pp. 54bl, 54cr, 105bl, 133t

Sonia Halliday: pp. 7ctl, 7ctr, 7cbl, 7cbr, 102tr, 117tl, 124l, 147t, 151tr